American Frankenstein

American Frankenstein

How the United States Created a Monster!

Like the creature in the Frankenstein story, the African American was created in the United States of America as an aberration of American citizenry, then relegated to a marginal existence in their homeland and condemned to a persistent socioeconomic struggle in the greatest country on earth.

Kyle Stanford Cramer

To order additional copies of this book, contact:
Xlibris Corporation
1-888-795-4274
www.Xlibris.com
Orders@Xlibris.com
74627

Dedication

American Frankenstein is dedicated to the tens of millions of African Americans who being deprived of dignity, have perished in this great land over the course of American history, and to the White Americans who joined with them in their pursuit of the American Dream: freedom, justice and equality for all.

Contents

Acknowledgements

While writing this book has been a long on again off again journey for a number of years, completing it was made possible by some very special people to whom I would like to extend my most gracious gratitude:

Joyce Pinjarkar, thank you for making time when you did not have time to spare. Your early review and insight helped me to massage the writing with more meaning and purpose.

Carol Dawley, thank you for your empathetic but stern perspective and diligent editing. You kept me focused on substance and helped me sharpen many points for clarity.

Robert Sideman, thank you for your input which showed me where I may have been too strongly influenced by the perspective of other writers. Also, your work on African Americans in Glencoe was "eye opening" for me and it's release could not have been timed better.

Wendy Serrino, your sharp intellect and keen social observations helped me to apply more critical analysis to everything written in this book. Thank you for keeping me honest.

Richard Stewart, you are truly a talented and patient illustrator. Thank you for enduring my numerous requests for renderings and re-renderings without much context other than cryptic notes.

Chandra Cramer, my wonderful wife whose intelligence, creativity and energy sparked the right ideas at the right time throughout this entire process. I am forever grateful to you.

Finally, thank you to the Xlibris staff: Randy Hughes, Jeremy Baring, Chile Gadingan, Amy Vallejos, Kay Benavides, Carolyn Gambito, Nica Silva and the Corrections department for your responsiveness during the submission, editing, production and marketing processes, it is much appreciated.

Preface

The Author's Perspective

Being inherently concerned with the plight of African Americans and disenfranchised by the seemingly impossible pursuit of rising them from a deep socioeconomic depression, I am frequently frustrated while seeing and experiencing the quality of life that America has to offer its upper middle class and affluent population, which has historically excluded, and is still largely foreign to most African Americans.

The majority of African Americans live in a subculture that suffers socially, intellectually, and economically and does not have equal access to opportunities in our land of plenty. While tens of millions of White Americans enjoy America's bounty more or less as a privileged rite of passage, millions of African Americans are left wallowing in the aftermath of one of mankind's most overt acts of exploitation toward one of its groups.

When you assess recently emerged and increasingly formal arguments by Black leaders like Renault Robinson and Maxine Waters regarding reparations for African Americans, you realize that it is not unreasonable for the United States to acknowledge past and current harm done to a significant portion of its people and to figure out some way to contribute to improving the condition of these people after hundreds of years of intentional exploitation, oppression, and neglect. However, direct financial reparation to individuals as compensation for the labor and toil of their African American ancestors is not the correct approach, since in most cases, those ancestors are long gone, their descendants would be difficult to qualify due to a variety of documentation issues described here in the chapter devoted to slavery, and direct links to discrimination and oppression can be subjective.

However, when you explore U.S. history as it relates to African Americans, it becomes absurd not to at least consider some form of reconstruction for American people of African descent, who have been and still are the most dejected and unaccepted people in the United States, which has resulted in loss of life, health, happiness, and opportunity in the greatest country and during the greatest period of progress in the recorded history of man. You cannot put a price on what has been forever lost to African Americans.

In *American Frankenstein* (forthcoming), I do not make light of other modern-day human offenses toward American Indians, Jews, Japanese, and others, but shed light on the United States government's neglect of a people who have, for hundreds of years, been systematically exploited, oppressed, physically and psychically abused, left out, and economically and socially marginalized more than any other group in the past few thousand years. While other groups may have lost life, limb, property, and the pursuit of happiness, the African American population has lost all of this, but, more devastating, it has lost itself.

Introduction

A Mind Is a Horrible Thing to Waste

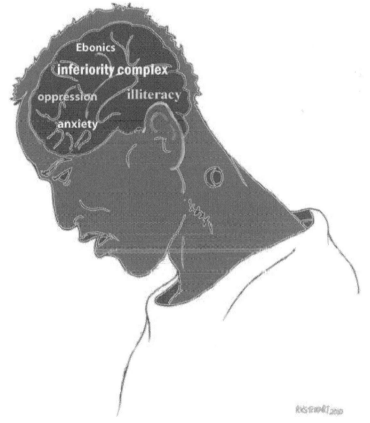

I once was a five-year-old Black boy growing up in the Ida B. Wells housing project on the south side of Chicago. The year was 1963, and on this particular day, my preschool is visited by Officer Friendly, who was a police officer in the Chicago Police Department delivering the Officer Friendly Program message to

Chicago elementary schoolchildren. The officer was professional in his appearance, an enthusiastic young man, and he was White, as nearly all Chicago policemen were in those days. Officer Friendly eloquently presented useful tips to the children on how to avoid Stranger Danger and Chester the Molester. The officer then concluded his visit by offering each child a gift, which was a plastic sheriff's badge pin. I put my pin on and wore it proudly for the rest of the school day and later upon returning home.

Coincidently that day, the evening news was broadcasting images from Birmingham, Alabama, of policemen turning back civil rights protesters who had assembled during a march. As I crossed paths with the family television, the images stopped me in my tracks. What I saw were hundreds of Officer Friendlies violently attacking thousands of people who looked like me. I observed the wrestling and beatings, the police dog attacks, and the intense brutality against Black men, women, and children. I remember specifically focusing on a boy, not much older than myself, rolling down the street by the force of water from a fire hose. I stood in front of the television stunned, confused, and perplexed by what I was seeing, contrasted by the friendly officer I experienced earlier in the day. It became painfully clear to me that because of the color of my skin, Officer Friendly, who had earned my trust and respect less than eight hours ago, could become very unfriendly.

That was the day that *it* happened to me. The *it* that I am referring to is a split consciousness that has historically and consistently developed in Blacks growing up in the United States of America who were traumatically exposed to the reality of race. It is a consciousness where, on one hand, you have your consciousness, which is who you inherently are at your core being, your soul. On the other hand, you have a consciousness where you look at yourself as a Black person through the eyes of the world around you.

This double consciousness casts a persistent scrutinizing shadow on everything you do, and everything you say, wherever you go. It is a dysfunctional consciousness that has plagued African Americans and negatively affected their mental and physical health for hundreds of years. This condition was described by W. E. B. Dubois, the great Black historian and scholar, as "Twosome" in his book entitled *The Souls of Black Folk* published in 1903. W. E. B. Dubois describes the phenomena, its effect on Black America, and African American's desire to be lifted from under the weight of this psychological burden in order to more productively and constructively pursue the American dream.[1]

Since my early childhood development and adolescence years occurred during the 1960s, I am among the last generations of African Americans who can directly associate their thoughts, both conscious and subconscious, to racially induced memories and experiences. My mental conditioning was nourished on a poor diet of derogatory imagery of African Americans; ill-intended audio, video, and written news media; and a variety of environmental factors that reinforced the introjections of negative stereotypes associated with a downtrodden race of people.

Growing up under the strength of these negative psychological influences certainly had an impact on my self-esteem and ability to envision entering the world in pursuit of a bright and productive future full of positive possibilities. While I have done well by the standard from where I have come, I'll never know how far I might have gone if not under the burden of the psychological baggage that I have carried every step of the way.

There has never been one introduction, job interview, business meeting, company outing, coworker wedding, performance review, mentoring session, or other interactions, where I was not, to some degree, preoccupied with the color of my skin and how it is being perceived by those around me, and what subsequent judgments they are making based on their preconceived notions.

Furthermore, I can list dozens of remarks and actions of Whites in these many encounters that exacerbated this inner discomfort and further fueled its flare-up as a result of their subtle acts of

---

[1] W.E.B. Dubois, *The Souls of Black Folk* (Chicago: A.C McClurg & Co.,1903)

rejection or prejudice. As a result, I have, on multiple occasions, remained silent when I knew the answer, stepped back and not up, held back when speaking up was in order, followed when I was in the best position to lead, and so on. This is not to say that I have performed this way every time, but that the weight of the psychological baggage can, at times, become so heavy that as a result of the shear mental exhaustion of this daily dilemma, you begin to calculate your actions and pick and choose those occasions where the benefit of action outweighs the perceived risk. This is unfortunate competitively since most who are not African American are wheeling and dealing free of this particular internal, self-limiting psychological condition.

This split consciousness condition "Twosome" that causes African Americans to question their worth and their abilities is the foundation for my premise that the current socioeconomical condition of a critical mass of African Americans today is directly attributable to the more than four hundred years, of generation after generation, of African Americans growing up in a racially hostile environment that induces this mental dysfunction. **For if you are made to believe that your life has little meaning or value, then your actions and your behavior will tend to produce results that reflect the way you think about yourself.**

After the Egyptian and Indian, the Greek and Roman, the Teuton and Mongolian, the Negro is a sort of seventh son, born with a veil, and gifted with second-sight in this American world,—a world which yields him no true self-consciousness, but only lets him see himself through the revelation of the other world. It is a peculiar sensation, this double-consciousness, this sense of always looking at one's self through the eyes of others, of measuring one's soul by the tape of a world that looks on in amused contempt and pity. One ever feels his twoness,—an American, a Negro; two souls, two thoughts, two un-reconciled strivings; two warring ideals in one dark body, whose dogged strength alone keeps it from being torn asunder.

—W. E. B. Dubois, *The Souls of Black Folk*

American Frankenstein is a perspective written as a timely response to the need for current-day Americans to revisit the history and the variety of experiences and realities of the Black existence in America. Until recently, the possibility of a serious attempt to reconstruct African Americans would have fallen on deaf ears, if not ignored completely, as our country's White majority has generally not been ready or willing to acknowledge or accept the root causes of the African American condition. *American Frankenstein* emphasizes the cause-and-effect connection between the deprived blighted history that Blacks have endured in America and the resulting self-destructive, hopeless existence of many African Americans today.

The book provides a reflective analysis for folks old enough to remember the highlights of the civil rights era and the consciousness it raised within White America about the unfairness in our society. It also provides context for younger readers for whom the only connection to these issues is sketchy accounts in history books and "politically correct" periodic television programming during Black History Month.

I aim to substantiate why reconstruction is required now, before it is too late, which is directly targeted at the segment of society born in the 1970s or later, and the immigrant segments of society causing "the browning of America." These citizens and foreigners have no direct exposure to and memory of the trying times endured by African Americans who came before them. In addition, time is quickly moving forward and closing the chapter on the experiences that resulted in today's Black reality in America. While there will always be historical references to these past events, society will eventually view it as just that—historical references to past events rather than root causes of the Black condition.

American Frankenstein paints a clear picture of the causal factors resulting in today's African American reality, which, at a minimum, should educate the masses on root causes for the African American condition and why African Americans represent either a vastly untapped pool of American human capital or a huge catalyst in America's downward social spiral.

The Issue

Socioeconomic Disparity

In Malcolm Gladwell's book *Outliers*, he presents very remarkable patterns generally associated with success. Malcolm Gladwell succinctly identifies factors that are clearly out of an individual's control but are directly related to their ability to be successful. Malcolm Gladwell writes and I quote,

> People don't rise from nothing. We do owe something to parentage and patronage. The people who stand before kings may look like they did it all themselves. But in fact they are invariably the beneficiaries of hidden advantages and extraordinary opportunities and cultural legacies that allow them to learn and work hard and make sense of the world in ways others cannot. It makes a difference where and when we grew up. The culture we belong to and the legacies passed down by our forebears shape the patterns of our achievement in ways we cannot begin to imagine. It's not enough to ask what successful people are like, in other words. It is only by asking where they are from that we can unravel the logic behind who succeeds and who doesn't.[2]

African Americans have been in the United States of America (USA) for over four hundred years. Slavery has been abolished for 145 years. The United States has grown over the last one hundred years to become the wealthiest and greatest country in the world. While African Americans were fortunate enough to have been in the United States before this explosion of economic growth, power, and prosperity, the African American community has not significantly participated in or benefited from this tremendous wealth-creating economic engine, which has created and passed down great opportunities to fellow White Americans for hundreds of years.

The depressed socioeconomic reality of the critical mass of African Americans today is the result of one of only two possibilities:

1. African Americans are inherently inferior and are intellectually incapable of initiating the processes and practices involved in producing the goods and services demanded by our society and the world, which thereby, create wealth.

---

2. Malcolm Gladwell (born September 3, 1963) is a Canadian journalist, author, and pop sociologist based in New York City. He is a staff writer for the *New Yorker* and is best known for his books *The Tipping Point* (2000), *Blink* (2005), *Outliers* (2008)

2. Or, for nearly four hundred years, African Americans have been automatically marginalized, held down, and shut out of the opportunities leading to success in the production of goods and services in United States of America, thereby suppressing their ability for wealth creation.

The following charts illustrate the disparity between African Americans as a percent of the population compared to the economic growth of the United States and the relative economic growth of the African American community over the same period of time. From the charts, it is clear to see that during the past 125 years of U.S. wealth creation, African Americans have consistently constituted around 12 percent of the U.S. population, but their 2008 economic participation is less than 2 percent of the total wealth created in the United States.

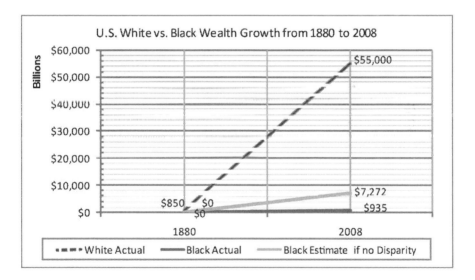

Source: Agricultural History, Vol. 67, No. 1 (Winter, 1993), pp. 1–15; U.S. Census Reports

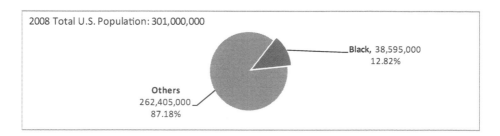

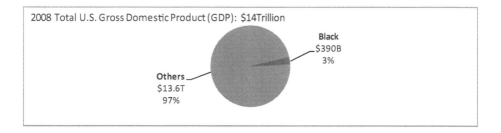

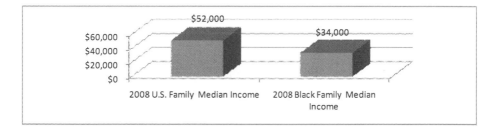

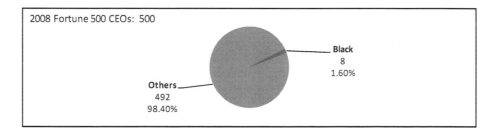

Source for preceding graphs: U.S. Census Reports; Black Enterprise

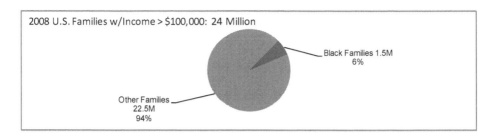

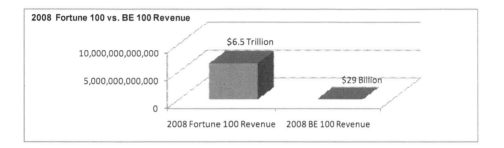

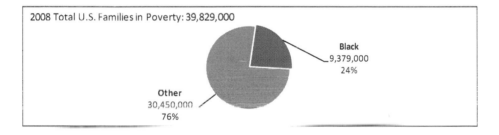

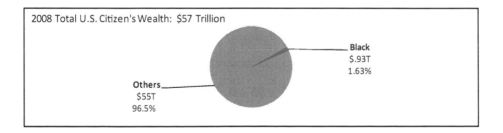

Source for preceding graphs: U.S. Census Reports; Black Enterprise

This socioeconomic disparity is not just about economic success but also the health and welfare of virtually an entire group of people. To this day, as a legacy of slavery, racial discrimination, and oppression, African Americans experience a dramatically worsened quality of life and general health conditions. Blacks have significantly higher mortality rates from cardiovascular disease, most cancers, diabetes, HIV, unintentional injuries, pregnancy, sudden infant death syndrome, and homicide than do Whites.

These disparities are sometimes rationalized on the basis of genetic differences despite strong evidence that genetic variances between all humans are insignificant. Conversely, there is much evidence to support the position that racial differences in socioeconomic status are the leading causes of these livelihood and health disparities. So even if the health of a Black person of low socioeconomic status has not yet been affected, there is likely to be a family member with, or at greater risk for ill health.

Even affluent Blacks living in a community of low socioeconomic status are at higher risk of cardiovascular mortality independent of their socioeconomic standing due to exposure to harmful environmental factors.

The primary factors contributing to the perpetuation of race-based socioeconomic disparities include the following:

1. Institutionalized racism that creates disadvantages for African Americans. Institutionalized racism manifest itself in racial inequities in employment, housing, education, health care, and the criminal justice system and is reinforced by racist beliefs inherent in a prejudiced society.
2. Individual racism, including unconscious preconceived bias. This is also manifested through discrimination in housing, banking and employment, racial profiling by police (of all races), harsher sentencing for African American defendants, lower educational expectations for Black students at all levels, and unequal medical treatment also known as medical racism.

3. Racial discrimination and biased treatment in society as a whole against African Americans. This enables racial stereotypes to contribute to voting patterns and social practices that, in turn, reinforce institutionalized and individual racism and continue the cycle of discrimination and alienation.

4. Internalized racism causes cognitive dissonance and affects an individual's own actions and behavior. Internalized racism is the introjections of racial stereotypes by African American members upon themselves causing a "self-hate" behavior to emerge, contributing to self-doubt, poor academic performance, depression, Black-on-Black crime, substance and sex abuse, dropout rates, and other high-risk behaviors.

Each of these factors reinforces the others with oppressive results. In addition, the social and cultural marginalization caused by segregation and alienation also contributes to substandard housing, underfunded public schools, joblessness, higher exposure to crime, environmental hazards, and, in short, loss of hope, which may be the most debilitating disadvantage of them all.

While there are far more poor White than Black people in the United States, the greater impact of poverty on African Americans is due to the fact that Blacks are disproportionately poor and more highly likely than their White counterparts to live in high-poverty communities.

Low-income children living in racially segregated communities typically attend schools where risk factors are highly concentrated. As a result, these children are more likely to be exposed to crime, sex, violence, and drug trafficking at a very young age, and they are less likely to be exposed to successful role models or professional social networks that frequently facilitate upward mobility.

The cumulative toll of these risk factors has been devastating to Black individuals, families, and communities across our nation and has prevented Blacks from participating in the magnificent creation of wealth enjoyed by others.

The following table reveals the results of this economic disparity for African Americans. The top one hundred companies owned and operated by African Americans combined are smaller than Coca-Cola, which is only one company on the Fortune 500 list.

2008 BE 100 Sales by Industry	%	Sales ($M)
Auto Dealers	31.10%	$8,932
Other	13.80%	$3,958
Manufacturing	13.70%	$3,941
Technology	11.20%	$3,227
Food & Beverage	9.20%	$2,660
Energy	6.10%	$1,754
Media	4.50%	$1,304
Construction	3.40%	$973
Transportation	2.90%	$828
Computer/Office Products	1.80%	$509
Security or Janitorial Maint.	0.90%	$271
Telecommunications	0.50%	$153
Entertainment	0.40%	$105
Healthcare	0.30%	$99
Healthcare & Beauty Aids	0.20%	$48
Source: Black Enterprise	100.00%	$28,763
Coca Cola	100.00%	$28,857

The following facts list some of the results ultimately rendered from the ongoing social and economic disparity experienced by America's Black population:

- Net worth of Black families $6,100—Net worth of White families $67,000. *Report from National Urban League, 2006*
- Only 41% of Black men graduate from high school in the United States. *Schott Foundation for Public Education*

- In Chicago, only 30% of Black males graduate from high school, of these only 3% of them obtain a bachelor's degree by the time they are 25.*Schott Foundation for Public Education/National Student Clearinghouse/Study by Consortium on Chicago School Research at the University of Chicago*
- 69% of Black children in America cannot read at grade level in the 4th grade, compared with 29% among White children. *National Association of Educational Progress*
- 45% of Black children live below the poverty line, compared with 16% of White youngsters. *Two Nations by Andrew Hacker*
- In 2000, 65% of Black male high-school dropouts in their 20's were jobless *2000 Census data.*
- The Black male homicide rate is seven times the White male rate.
- Black women are 18 times more likely to be raped than White women.
- *The Justice Department* estimates that one out of every 21 Black men can expect to be murdered, a death rate double that of U. S. soldiers in World War II.
- A young Black male in America is more likely to die from gun fire than was any soldier during the Vietnam War.
- While constituting roughly 12% of the total population, Black America represents almost 26% of America's poor in 2010.
- 67% of Black children (up from 17% in 1967) are born out of wedlock.
- Black men earn 67% of what White men earn.
- 53% of Black men aged 25-34 are either unemployed or earn too little to lift a family of four from poverty.
- Blacks comprise only 3.2% of lawyers, less than 3% of doctors, and less than 1% of architects.

While some African Americans are benefiting from the results of the Civil Rights Movement, affirmative action initiatives, and the overall improvement in equality, fairness and openness in the United States society, the masses of African Americans are experiencing increasingly negative socioeconomic statistics, which will worsen until a national recognition of the root causes enables us to "cure" the chronic dysfunction in the African American community.

The Frankenstein Analogy

The Frankenstein Analogy[3] occurred to me while watching the original Frankenstein movies, when I realized that the creature that Dr. Frankenstein created was not inherently bad, but was made

---

[3]   The Frankenstein analogy relates Dr. Frankenstein to the U.S. government, law enforcement and society, and the Frankenstein creature to African Americans, and the misguided pursuits of the former and affliction of the later.

dysfunctional by the way he was handled by Dr. Frankenstein, Dr. Frankenstein's assistant, and society.

As Dr. Frankenstein diligently and feverishly implemented his plan to create life, he went out into the world and cobbled together parts of people. Some parts from laboratories, some from people whose corpses were robbed from their graves, some of whom were newly dead. The people from which Dr. Frankenstein acquired body parts were varied and mismatched. He acquired an abnormal brain from one source, a good heart from another, and other pieces and parts from still others. Dr. Frankenstein fulfilled his ambition when he suddenly struck life into this being that was concocted as an aberration of different people from different places.

As the creature came to life, he was born into a state of total confusion. He had no idea who he was, or from where he came. He knew not how to communicate, behave, or assimilate. In addition, the creature was "abnormal," in that he did not fit the cultural and social norm of what society thought people should look and act like. As a result, the creature was immediately misunderstood, mishandled, neglected, and ultimately outcast from society. The creature could have been a great asset to Dr. Frankenstein and his community but immediately became a monster to be hated, scrutinized, and relegated to a subhuman existence. Even Dr. Frankenstein and his assistant did not know how to interpret the peculiar communication attempts and needs of the creature, which led to their subsequent actions of hostility, neglect, and abandonment of the creature.

As the creature emerged into society, matters got worse. The creature was ill-equipped intellectually, socially, culturally, emotionally, and spiritually to navigate his way through the interactions in society in a way that would enable him to fit in, be appreciated, and excel. Instead of finding his way into a constructive and productive existence, the creature roamed aimlessly into society looking naively for where he belonged, only to encounter society's rejection-filled wrath every step along the creature's path.

Society immediately feared and rejected the creature's differences. The creature had an unappealing appearance by society's standards, and he was an anomaly in a society that conformed to very specific physical human characteristics and social norms. The creature was not educated, trained, or developed in any of the disciplines of value to the society and could not read, write, or properly speak the language of the society. In addition, the creature did not understand the cultural norms and values of the society. So as the creature encountered people, many times in the most innocent way, they were prejudiced by his overall presence, demeanor, and communication pattern. So they attacked him, degraded him, tried to run him out of town, and/or kill him. In some instances, the creature would be attempting to provide assistance to people in his awkward and feeble way, but with a good heart. These acts requiring closeness would be misinterpreted as an aggressive threat, and the creature would be quickly made to know that his presence was neither welcomed nor wanted.

Frankenstein's creature only found peace and happiness when he stumbled across a man playing a violin who happened to be blind. The sweet sound of the blind man's violin attracted the creature through the woods to the blind man's cabin. The blind man heard the creature at his door and invited him in without the visual ability to judge or reject the creature based on his physical differences.

As the blind man learned of the creature's inability to communicate, he taught him to speak. He also taught the creature the concept of good and bad and the concept of friendship. The blind man and the creature became good friends and enjoyed music, wine, and cigars together. The creature finally felt accepted and where he belonged.

It was not until the blind man's neighbors passed by and discovered the creature in the blind man's presence that the creature became unacceptable. The neighbors instantly rejected the creature's apparent civilized behavior and the blind man's acceptance of the creature. Then all hell broke loose again.

The Frankenstein analogy is that the United States government and society (Dr. Frankenstein) created the African American (the creature) in an environment where—because of the African American's former slave status—physical differences, communication pattern, and culture, they were mishandled and made dysfunctional, then relegated to a marginal existence in the Great American society, where they have wallowed ever since.

The African American has no past before America since their country of origin, language, religion, and names were stripped from them. In addition, the African American became a blend of many different people from various parts of the world, including African nations, European nations, and American Indians. Then, added to this are the debilitating effects of a long history of slavery, oppression, lynching, and discrimination. So like the creature in the Frankenstein story, the African American was created as the result of a mix of people cobbled together from many parts, not really knowing who they are or from whence they came, and subsequently abused, rejected, and outcast in society.

As with Dr. Frankenstein's creature, African Americans have been aimlessly trying to find their way in society, trying to fit in, to improve themselves, to contribute to society, and to improve their quality of life. Likewise, as with Dr. Frankenstein's creature, the African American's plight has been filled with hatred, mistrust, neglect, and outright violent rejection.

Society conjured up perceptions that demonized and criminalized the Black man and imagined him as a constant threat to the virtue of White women. For years, society bestowed an inferior intellectual character and spiritual status on the African American and relegated them to second-class citizen status, capable only of menial, labor-intensive, low-wage employment.

While African Americans strived to assimilate into society by acquiring education, improving their proper use of English, treating their hair making it straighter, and generally trying to look and act more acceptable in the eyes of White America, they were still, by and large, unaccepted and unappreciated. It did not matter what

African Americans did, they were generally rejected just as the creature was in the Frankenstein story.

To further complicate the modern-day African American, you have anomalies like President Barack Obama, Oprah Winfrey, Colin Powell, Clarence Thomas, Ben Carson, Cornell West, and Condoleezza Rice among many other very successful and/or highly educated and often wealthy African American individuals, while at the same time, you have a race that possess the highest percentages of negative economic and social statistics tracked today.

Across the spectrum of successful and unsuccessful African Americans, you have a societal-induced damaged sense of self resulting in a self-hate that causes Blacks to gravitate toward Whiteness as illustrated by the physical evolution of Michael Jackson, as an extreme example. This ingrained behavioral dysfunction also causes Blacks to sabotage their communities and lives by making poor choices resulting from the low self-esteem experienced by many. This manifests itself in a lack of vision of future possibilities and results in drug abuse, unsafe sex, crime, destruction of property, littering and loitering, and other acts of low morale character.

The irony is that, as with Frankenstein's creature, African Americans possess the potential to be a plentiful source of human capital for the nation, its communities and institutions, and to society at large. If care and fairness had replaced hatred and bigotry over the last few hundred years, the African American would have developed into one of the country's greatest human assets. The value of this would be felt everywhere throughout the nation as the quality of character, education, and life of millions of African Americans today would reflect the goodwill of America rather than America's history of oppression and neglect.

You can argue that had the United States been fair and equitable toward its African American population, which represents approximately 13 percent of society, that on average, every aspect of society would have been improved simply as a result of the productivity factor derived from millions of people rendered more productive. This translates into improved goods and services across all spectrums of the U.S. commercial and public institutions, as a higher quality of more educated African Americans in the workplace would be better calibrated for high-quality performance.

The United States has made attempts to "equalize" Black life in America by providing children equal access to education, granting equal access to public facilities for everyone, and establishing affirmative action to generate greater workplace and business opportunities for African Americans and others. The following chapters will describe how and why these efforts have been anemic when compared to the depth in which the African American has been psychologically and socioeconomically injured as a result of their history in America.

A root-cause analysis is required to truly understand the magnitude of damage done to African Americans, and only then can deeply penetrating and meaningful initiatives be conceived to address and cure the variety of ailments that plague the Black community. This root-cause understanding would also be enlightening to all people of America so that they can begin to understand the cause-and-effect reality of the Black community and why the approach of "treating symptoms," as we have done in the past, will never produce the broad-reaching results we desire. We have to figure out how to "cure" the dysfunction.

The question is, has the potential, spirit, ambition, and goodness been squashed out of a people by their master who created then neglected them, leaving them to wallow aimlessly and dysfunctionally through life without recourse as with Dr. Frankenstein's creature? Or, is there enough understanding and compassion left in the American society to recognize the error of its ways toward a group of its people, and enough esteem and desire left in the critical mass of African Americans, such that an earnest attempt by both to correct for past indiscretions can produce a constructive and meaningful pursuit to elevate the quality of life for the African American population, who has earned it through hundreds of years of loyalty, toil, and strife?

Slavery

The Main Ingredient

In 1530, Juan de la Barrera, a slave merchant, began transporting slaves directly from Africa to North America (slaves previously passed through Europe first). His venture proved very profitable, and his lead was quickly followed by other slave traders.

Needless to say, the enslavement of Blacks in America, enabled by government for the next 335 years, became by far the most crippling factor imposed on these Americans in the new world full of tremendous opportunity.

The dehumanizing process of capturing, shackling, inspecting, cargoing, shipping, and selling slaves would have surely been a permanently traumatic experience for millions of Africans tightly stuffed into the belly of ships for a two-month voyage across the ocean.

The loss of identity associated with losing one's language, name, family, religion, culture, and community would surely rob people of their dignity and sense of self-worth.

To be chained and herded like cattle while being led to an auction where you're inspected from head to toe and subjected to the fierce scrutiny and criticism of other human beings, who are obviously determining your value to a prospective owner, was a process fit for animals, not humans. Then to be displayed on the auction block, as the subject of this socio-commercial event while onlookers bid and joke and generally make business and entertainment at the expense of human dignity, represents the worse of the detrimental ways humans can treat one another.

Being forced into hard labor was sheer hell for the initial generations of African slaves, who were controlled by chains and whips. Slaves would be harshly punished for not being productive enough, or for seemingly stepping out of line when the slaves could not know where the line was, since they did not understand the language being used to instruct their activity.

To add to the suffering of slaves who found love or procreated under these extreme circumstances, loved ones and children were regularly taken and sent to the auction block and sold to the highest bidder never to be heard from again.

Each time a slave changed masters, the slave's name changed as well, making it difficult for family members to track them even if they could. Not only were slaves initially removed from their homeland and family name and structures, but for 350 years, they were not allowed to develop or continue strong family relationships and ties.

Because slaves were property rather than free people, slave births and deaths were not documented or recorded in any jurisdiction causing a permanent sever in the lineage of millions of African Americans.

During slavery, it was customary for White slave owners to conduct public displays of executions, whippings, brandings, and various other severe forms of punishment. Slaves from various plantations would be assembled specifically to witness the punishment as an example of the White master's absolute authority over the life and death of their slaves. Supporting these horrific practices was the idea that Blacks were not really human beings and were not entitled to the rights of life or liberty beyond what their master saw fit to grant.

As time moved on, the slavery establishment became more mature and refined in its operation and oppressive methods. Slaves were unable to look White people in the eye, for direct eye contact with Whites indicated lack of deference and subjected slaves to beatings. Slaves were unable to learn to read since it became important to keep slaves as ignorant as possible while allowing Whites to pretend that slaves were inherently intellectually inferior due to their lack of knowledge. Slaves who could speak perfectly good English were forced to speak in demeaning ways and trained their children to speak "improperly" as a survival tactic. By speaking ignorantly automatically, you protect yourself when encountering Whites since they would not think the slave was getting too smart or becoming a threat.

Female slaves were the regular victims of rape by their master, fieldsman, or White men in general who found the opportunity to satisfy their sexual appetite at the slave woman's expense. The routine rape of slave women and girls created another dynamic that would further perpetuate the destruction of the Black family.

Consider the dynamic created between Black men and women as women are repeatedly raped or whipped while the female's father, brother, husband, lover, or friend was left powerless to act on behalf of his daughter, sister, wife, lover, or friend.

Nothing in the world can make a man feel less than a man than his inability to protect his woman or loved ones. Slave men were subjected to over 350 years of this condition and were periodically injured or killed when reacting to the normal natural warrior instinct to protect or escape. In many cases, raped slave women produced mulatto children who became slave children of the masters. The proliferation of rape was so widespread that over the course of slavery, the color of African Americans transformed from Black to every shade in between black and white.

The mulatto children born to slave women, that would be fathered by the White slave master or field hands, would have no meaningful relationship with their fathers and sometimes be completely ignored, denied, or sold off since they were in fact slaves as well and, an in some cases, an embarrassment to the slave master's wife.

For hundreds of years, only the strongest self-disciplined men and women could endure slavery year after year without any hope of freedom and remain sane and at peace. Otherwise, you had to have a "slave mentality," which was a mind-set that accepted your slave condition as the reality of your life and you tried to be a good slave rather than a discontent one. In either case, you had to keep your head down and do your work and never act out against the world of inhumane treatment going on around you.

For many less disciplined and high-spirited discontent individuals, slavery represented an often fatal challenge. These individuals reacted in ways that more often than not cost them life, limb, or isolation. If caught conspiring or attempting to escape, or performing any other unacceptable behavior such as lashing out or striking a White person, this slave could expect to pay a maximum penalty.

Slaves were given the meat scraps leftover from the animals slaughtered for sale or from the preparation of the master family's meals. These items were essentially garbage and included pig feet, chitterlings (pig guts), pigtails, pig ears, chicken necks, animal organs, and other undesirable animal parts. The slaves would prepare grain products and combine them with whatever meat scraps they could get. Bad food, hard work, and inhumane living conditions perpetuated an overall negative health and life span condition for many slaves. In addition, a debilitating mental state from psychological abuse and low self-esteem developed within individuals who lived under such conditions while observing the bountiful life to be had by Whites of the same county, town, and plantation. This inferior mental state was more often than not passed on to the slave children for generations to come.

The destruction of families of African descent during nearly four hundred years of slavery took a tremendous toll on the sense of heritage, legacy, and pride associated with family structures and lineage. Unlike most people of the United States, African Americans can't discuss with pride the "old country" where their family tree originates. Most can only go back a few generations to a southern U.S. state. In fact, most Blacks' surnames are completely irrelevant since they were arbitrarily assigned based on who their ancestor's slave master was and changed whenever their ancestors were sold to a new master. This is why some Black activist like Malcolm X replaced his surname *Little* with the letter *X*. The surname of most African Americans today is simply the name of the White slave master who owned their ancestor at the time of the Emancipation Proclamation. Their ancestors' names before that are largely unknown.

For hundreds of years during slavery, so many family connections were severely obliterated due to separating slave family members, selling and renaming slaves, runaway slaves, and overt slave lynching and murder, that it's surprising that any sense of family ties and dignity exists within African American families today at all.

Since slaves were considered chattel, "live" property, no different than horses and mules, there were no certificates of birth or death, no marriage certificates or other public records, making it difficult to understand, identify, and track relationships and connections between family members for many generations.

Slavery perpetuated disjointed families with severely deteriorated values and relationship issues, which continue to impact the African American family today. No remedy has been seriously conceived, let alone implemented to begin to rebuild the African American heritage and family structure broken and severely damaged by the practice of slavery.

During slavery, Blacks had to learn a foreign language while fulfilling the need to appear inferior and demonstrating submission as a survival mechanism. The speech patterns that resulted from broken English and subservient behavior among African slaves would form the foundation of the dialect spoken by many African Americans today.

For hundreds of years, Blacks had to suppress their ability to speak proper English for fear of offending Whites. If it were known that a Black was attempting to learn to read or write, that could mean death or, at the very least, a lashing. It was extremely important for White Southerners particularly to maintain control over Blacks by keeping them ignorant and feeling inferior, as well as to justify Whites' feelings of superiority while Blacks around them behaved subserviently.

Throughout slavery and for several years after, Black elders would swiftly correct the learning behavior of Black youth when the youngsters displayed speech or intellectual prowess unfitting for a Black. To survive in White America, Blacks had to maintain their ignorant presentation in both language and demeanor. As years rolled on, this tendency to thwart Black intellect manifested itself automatically and persistently as a cultural trait of African Americans. What began as a defense and survival mechanism while speaking to Whites evolved over hundreds of years into the dysfunctional cultural norm of African American dialect that today we call Ebonics.

Even today in predominantly Black communities, the norm is to dissuade individuals from talking or appearing too "proper" in their manner or for "acting White." Unfortunately, the survival tactic of displaying inferior intelligence in the past has manifested itself into a cultural trait where today, it is not "cool" to speak, look, or act like you are smart, and in fact, becoming smart can make you an outcast and a target and get you bullied, ostracized, or even killed in some Black communities.

Slavery possibly bred qualities of leadership and industriousness out of the slave population. The most spirited and charismatic of slaves became the targets of regular whippings, lynching, and isolation. These were the slaves who were not able to contain themselves within the confines of slavery and would act out to their demise. They would attempt to run away, show contempt, become unruly, try to organize, or do other inappropriate behavior. These slaves were likely singled out and controlled and were not as readily available for procreating. After three hundred and fifty years of this "unintentional breeding," genetic traits associated with leadership and ingenuity may have, to some degree, been systematically extricated from the African American population.

On the other hand, character traits associated with being a person of limited assertiveness and ambition may have been bred into the slave population over hundreds of years because this is the behavior that was required to survive.

The result of the raping of slave women and girls would create, among other things, a very colorfully diverse population of slaves. As rape continued and its mulatto offspring came of age and procreated as well, being Black became more than a literal interpretation of one's pigment. Being Black became defined as anyone with a single drop of Black blood in his or her bloodline. This "pure White" concept has done significant harm in its own right to not only the Black community but also to people of color throughout the world. Anyone not light enough to pass for

White was automatically considered intellectually and socially inferior in the White mainstream, regardless of economic status or character.

The irrationality of the "pure White" concept is so extreme that it is perplexing how anyone finds reason in it at all. Identifying someone with white skin as Black is as ridiculous as identifying someone with black skin as White. When a pure White Anglo-Saxon has a child with a pure African, the child is both White and Black.

This affinity toward Whiteness has detrimentally impacted the Black community internally as well. Lighter-skinned Blacks have always received preferential treatment within the Black community. They've been labeled more attractive, and they have enjoyed greater success than their darker brothers and sisters. This is due to their less threatening appearance in the White society,[4] as well as Black's internal conditioning by the White society causing even Blacks to look at themselves negatively for being dark. The fact of the matter has always been this: smart and dim-witted people as well as good and bad people come in all colors.

Today, the health and life span of many Blacks are largely victimized by the eating habits passed down from slavery. The regular diet of many African American families is low in nutritional value and high in fat and sodium, which are two of the primary contributors to heart disease. When you combine poor nutrition with the working conditions that have been historically made available to Blacks, along with the sociopsychological impairments of many Blacks, it begins to make sense why certain medical conditions seem to occur more within the Black community. Working at hard labor in an oftentimes unclean or unsafe environment while on a poor diet and with mental health conditions is a recipe for ill health and/or a short life.

---

[4]   Consider Senator Harry Reid's comment regarding the electability of Barack Obama as president: "Obama had a chance of winning because he was both "light-skinned" and didn't speak with a "negro dialect."

It is a reasonable conclusion that the higher rate of chronic health conditions among Blacks is partly attributable to the fact that government-enabled slavery, racism, and discrimination, over an extended period of time, has disproportionately exposed African Americans to health hazards due to environmental, lifestyle, and mental conditions that disproportionately embrace Blacks. Today, Black communities continue to be plagued with health issues resulting from a legacy of unhealthy food and inferior living environments.

Reconstruction

Failure to Launch

The assassination of President Abraham Lincoln was a lethal blow to the progress of postslavery Blacks. Under the leadership of President Lincoln, a progressive reconstruction program had begun to lift Blacks from the doldrums of slavery and second-class citizenship to a place where they would share in the political, social, educational, and economical benefits of the country.

In the late 1860s, Blacks were elected and appointed to political offices in numbers that would not be seen again until the 1970s, over a century later. President Lincoln's death was not only a tragic event for the country but also a devastating setback for the plight of African Americans as Lincoln's vision, leadership, and charisma were essential ingredients in persuading the ruling body to move the African American people forward. Lincoln had made the emancipated Negro the ward of the nation and had put in motion plans to bring them into full citizenship. It was to be a tremendous undertaking if fully implemented. With the stroke of the presidential pen, Lincoln erected millions of men, women, and children emasculated by hundreds of years of slavery, and then, suddenly, reborn as the result of war, to live and thrive among a resentful and angry population of former slave masters and Southern Whites.

After Lincoln's death, movements began to reverse the good work that had been done since slavery. Blacks with power and influence and in political offices were systematically targeted, threatened, and removed oftentimes violently from their positions of political influence. By 1900, virtually all Black political office holders[5] in positions of power and influence had been removed from U.S. state and local governments, particularly in South Carolina, where Whites aggressively strived to eliminate Black's political power and influence. South Carolinians desired to prolong the slave-master relationship between Blacks and Whites in an altered state. As a result, the progress achieved by African Americans was short-lived. Not long after the Confederacy's defeat, South Carolina instituted a new constitution that was designed with codes known as Jim Crow[6] to specifically control Blacks.

In 1865, President Andrew Johnson, who succeeded Lincoln, returned most land under federal control to their previous White

---

[5] There were over 1,500 African Americans in political office during Reconstruction (1865–1876). They all were Republicans. Source: Wikisource

[6] Jim Crow, a practice or policy of segregating or discriminating against Blacks in public places, public vehicles, or employment.

owners. Many African Americans were threatened with removal from the land that was granted to them following the Civil War. The freed slaves had no choice but to work as laborers or sharecroppers on once-again White-owned plantations. In addition, South Carolina's constitution of 1865 did not grant African Americans the right to vote, and it retained racial qualifications for the state legislature.

South Carolina's new constitution created the climate necessary for the pervasive enactment of Jim Crow. It effectively guaranteed White superiority over African Americans and denied African Americans social, economic, and political equality. Black voting declined, and they began to fail at securing political offices or enjoying equality under the law. The Black legislature of South Carolina had no respect from White citizens who refused to accept the reality of Black political influence. To make matters worse, the federal government did not intervene as Southern-state politicians intimidated Blacks out of office and passed laws stripping African Americans of their rights, including their right to vote.

The Freedmen's Bureau was established in 1865 to help freed slaves' transition into citizens of the United States of America. The bureau was designed to provide relief for Blacks and Whites who were left destitute by the Civil War. The Freedmen's Bureau was the "umbilical cord" needed to engage newly freed Blacks into American society by establishing schools, labor relations, and protection from violence and intimidation, particularly in the Southern states, where postwar hostilities were at their peak. Unfortunately, President Johnson vetoed the initial bill that would enact the bureau.

Consequently, Johnson's vetoes provoked Republicans to pass the Fourteenth Amendment, which aimed to guarantee the civil rights of all citizens, whatever their race, and to restrict the political power of former Confederates. Johnson denounced the proposed amendment because he believed it violated states' rights. In April 1866, the first Civil Rights Act, which was designed to guarantee equal civil rights to Blacks, was passed in spite of Johnson's veto. After the 1866 Congress was elected, Republicans maintained enough power to pass the reconstruction program.

The Freedmen's Bureau took responsibility for furnishing food and medical supplies to Blacks, most of whom were destitute. It was also concerned with the regulation of wages and working conditions of Blacks, the establishment and maintenance of schools for illiterate former slaves, and the control and distribution of lands abandoned by or confiscated from Southern proprietors. In addition, the bureau handled legal trials involving Blacks.

Emancipation was a liberating experience to former slaves representing autonomy and freedom from White control. Newly freed Blacks moved off of plantations to cities and sought out family members and loved ones from whom they had long since separated. They formed new institutions of learning and religion for literacy and spiritual support. In many parts of the South, Blacks strove for integrated access to public facilities.

In 1865 and 1866, newly freed African Americans began to sign labor contacts with planters to do field work in exchange for wages, housing, food, and clothing. These former slaves soon found the new system to be very similar to slavery. As a result, the labor system of sharecropping evolved and seemed preferable. Under sharecropping, landowners rented small parcels of land to Blacks for a percentage of the crop they harvested. The payment, unfortunately, was only enough to sustain a menial existence and survive, not get ahead.

In 1875, Congress passed a Civil Rights Act to bar segregation in public facilities. Blacks, however, sought not integration with Whites but freedom from White control and interference in their activities. A primary goal of freed slaves was to own land; however, most former slaves lacked the resources to buy land, and real property continued to be controlled by Whites.

To understand this period, you have to understand the "atmosphere" in the United States in the late 1860s: General Lee had surrendered, Lincoln had been assassinated, and President Johnson and the Congress were in constant disagreement; the Thirteenth, Fourteenth, and Fifteenth Amendments were either adopted or pending; raged White southern men were raiding and terrorizing the ex-slave population, and the entire South was awakening from the nightmare of the Civil War to a reality of ruins, poverty, and social revolution. [7]

Even in a hypothetical era of peace, collaborative neighbors, and communal wealth, the social, political, and economic uplift of 4,500,000 slaves to full participation in U.S. citizenship would have been a major achievement in its own right. So when you add hate-infused human conflict, former master-slave relationships, and postwar resentment to the inherent difficulties of a revolutionary social and political agenda, any strategy to fundamentally implement social reorder to equalize slaves was destined to failure if executed without adequate controls.

The Freedmen's Bureau denounced a principle in the South that Southerners believed, which was that life among free Negroes was simply unthinkable. As such, it was considered to be an experiment that could not be allowed to succeed. The agents that the bureau commissioned varied from unselfish philanthropists to bigots and thieves, and even though the average agent was better than the worst, it is always the one bad apple that spoils the whole bunch.

Finally, among all of this was the freed slave stranded in a land between friend and foe. African Americans had emerged from a slavery that classified the Black man and the mule together. The ex-slave knew full well that Southern White men had fought desperately to perpetuate slavery and continued to fight to sustain White superiority. Blacks during this time were inarticulate, had inferior attitudes and demeanor, and were frightened and tenuous at best.

This was the backdrop for the work of the Freedmen's Bureau from 1865 until 1869. To summarize the four years of the bureau's work, there were approximately nine hundred bureau agents scattered from Washington to Texas, overseeing

---

7. Dubois, W. E. B, *Black Reconstruction in America*, 1860-1880 (Free Press, 1999)

millions of former slaves. The activities of the bureau's agents fell mainly into seven categories:

1. The relief of physical suffering
2. The overseeing of labor
3. The buying and selling of land
4. The establishment of schools
5. The paying of bounties
6. The administration of justice
7. The financing of these activities

By the summer of 1869, over half a million patients had been treated by the bureau's physicians and surgeons in about sixty hospitals and asylums, over 21,000,000 food rations were distributed, and over 30,000 Black men were transported from the refuges and relief stations back to the farms to try sharecropping, a new form of slave labor. The largest element of success was the fact that the majority of the freedmen were willing and eager to work. As a result, contracts were written, and laborers and employers were connected throughout all of the plantation states.

The bureau essentially became a labor program and, under tough circumstances, became somewhat successful. Two obstacles normally confronted the bureau's officers:

1. The Southern White man who believed that slavery was right and was determined to disrupt the bureau's efforts.
2. The idle ex-slave who, after a lifetime of labor and toil, regarded freedom as a long-awaited rest.

The greatest success of the Freedmen's Bureau was the establishment of the free school system for the former slaves. By 1870, more than 150,000 children were in school. The South violently opposed Negro education, for the South believed that an educated Negro would become a threat. In fact, history does show that education bestowed on all kinds of men usually had, and always will have, an element of danger and revolution, of dissatisfaction and discontent. Nevertheless, every man still has a human right to become educated.

The Black colleges founded in these days included Fisk, Atlanta, Howard, and Hampton, and nearly $6,000,000 was expended in five years for related educational work. The Freedmen themselves contributed about $750,000 to these initiatives, the purchases of land and various other enterprises, which showed that ex-slaves were accumulating and handling capital. The primary source of Freedmen's income was from labor in the army and the pay and bounty as a soldier. Unfortunately, payments to Freedmen were so plagued with fraud that Congress put the whole process in the hands of the Freedmen's Bureau.

The least successful part of the Freedmen's Bureau's work was the exercise of its judicial functions, particularly in the South, where slavery was newly relinquished. To keep the Whites from overtly abusing the ex-slaves, and the ex-slaves from miscalculating their prominence and security while surrounded by hate-filled Southerners, created a challenging job at best. As former slaves were regularly intimidated, beaten, raped, and mutilated by angry and revengeful Southern White men, the bureau courts tended to become centers for punishing Whites, albeit not very successfully, and the regular civil courts regularly perpetuated the pseudoslavery of Blacks.

Nearly every law that politicians could devise was employed by the legislatures to reduce the ex-slave's full citizen stature and revert them back to slaves of the state, if not of individual owners. The Freedmen's Bureau officials, those of good intentions, strived to give the freed slaves a power and independence that the former slaves unfortunately could not use due to the overwhelming sentiment among Southern Whites to keep their position of superiority.

The Freedmen's Bureau set out to provide a variety of services that would help the freed slaves penetrate the socioeconomic systems and flourish within the United States. Many of their efforts were interrupted due to weak federal oversight, corruption, and the Southern culture. Unfortunately, most freed slaves remained in the South where hostility continued to brew fervently among disenfranchised White Southerners. Many White Southerners lost lives, land, slaves, and other resources and certainly did not want to lose their sense of superiority over the now-free Southern Black population. As a result of Southern White hostility and a lack of federal law enforcement, many of the Freedmen's Bureau efforts were not nearly as effective as intended.

By 1877, reconstruction had ended less than ten years since it began. White Democrats had regained nearly total control of the state legislatures across the South and had stripped all of the power and influence gained by Black men since the Emancipation Proclamation. Southern Whites then passed laws to substantially reduce the Black vote by making voter registration more complicated.

By 1908, nearly all Southern legislatures ratified new constitutions with amendments to disfranchise African Americans through poll taxes, property and residency requirements, and literacy tests. Although voting criteria was required of all voters, many states passed grandfather clauses to exempt White illiterates from literacy tests. The result was that Blacks were stripped of their rights to vote, serve on juries, or participate in other governing activities. In essence, the Black citizen's political voice had been annihilated.

The Freedmen's Bureau was the single most important governmental act that would produce positive conditions for former slaves. Unfortunately, the premature dismantling of much of the bureau after only four years was the initial and primary postslavery act of the United States government that abandoned the opportunity to support the "full citizenship" of the Negro through social and economic uplift and began the painful prolonged struggle of African Americans to scratch and scrape their way into the American economic system, which continues today, nearly 150 years since the end of slavery. You have to wonder how successful the bureau would have been if it had adequate backing and committed support from the U.S. government over a longer period of time.

While some good was accomplished by the Freedmen's Bureau in the form of schools for Blacks, distribution of property rights and legal representation, the organization was unfortunately riddled with unscrupulous characters who were involved for selfish gain.

Much of the resources targeted to freed slaves never reached them. While thousands of slaves did benefit from the resources of the Freedmen's Bureau, much of what they gained was quickly stolen, taken, or swindled away from them do to widespread illiteracy, ignorance, naivety, fear, and general lack of business sense, which was common across the Black population, all against a backdrop of racism, little or no resources, and sketchy legal representation, especially after the Freedmen's Bureau oversight ended.

During this post-Civil War era, many Blacks could not find work outside of plantations, making it difficult to earn a living and causing them to sometimes engage in petty theft, grand larceny, and robbery. Whites, on the other hand, were struggling to adjust to the new social order with Blacks and felt increasingly insecure about what they perceived as the inability of the Freedmen's Bureau to control newly freed Blacks. As a consequence, Whites periodically joined lynching parties as they saw mob violence as their best option to control the freedmen.

If you consider the good that was rendered from the short-lived and corrupted life of the Freedmen's Bureau, along with the temporary surge in Black political influence resulting in privileges for African Americans, including good schools, property ownership, etc., it becomes easy to see that had the Freedmen's Bureau's work been conducted in full force for four decades instead of four years and had the appropriate level of oversight and controls been instituted for effective administration and governance of the programs, much of the intent of the bureau would have been realized and its resources would have produced an upwardly mobile group of productive American citizens.

Likewise, had Reconstruction and the surge of Black political influence been allowed to continue and thrive, not for ten years but indefinitely, Blacks would have had an opportunity to enjoy early participation in the incubation of modern industries, major companies, and progressive communities. For even without the substantial support, resources, legal representation, and the like, some Blacks managed to eke out a living for themselves and a future for their children, and repeatedly made it possible for the next generation to do better than the last. This was accomplished by and large through menial jobs like doing laundry, cleaning homes, general labor and maintenance work, sharecropping, fishing, etc. Had these hardworking and resourceful people who consistently made something out of nothing had access to knowledge, capital, and unobstructed free market business opportunities, there is no telling where African Americans would be today.

Ex-slaves lived during a time where America's industrial glory and financial bounty was in its infancy and growing at an amazingly rapid rate. African Americans could have enjoyed being on the ground floor of every major industry that exists today. Because of the shortcomings of the Freedmen's Bureau and the lack of government protection and support, Blacks continued to be largely shut out of the American dream and all it represented, and as a result, fundamentally, there are no major enterprises founded by African Americans and virtually no African American heads of major enterprises today.

Forty Acres and a Mule

False Hope

After the Civil War, when the Emancipation Proclamation was executed, America attempted to do the right thing by the newly freed slaves by forming the Freedmen's Bureau to attend to the needs of these new and aimless citizens. The Freedmen's Bureau was established as part of the U.S. War Department by an act of Congress in March 1865. Its principal aim was to provide assistance to the newly emancipated Blacks of the South after the American Civil War to bring them into full citizenship.

The lands controlled by the Freedmen's Bureau, totaling about eight hundred thousand acres, were originally intended to be distributed to former slaves and to persons of proved loyalty to the Union, in lots not to exceed forty acres. Because of opposition among Whites in Southern legislatures, this plan was abandoned, and much of the land was returned to the former plantation owners, causing severe disappointment to Blacks, who had hoped to establish themselves as independent farmers. The weak commitment and oversight of the United States government eventually allowed the support and resources behind the Freedmen's Bureau to subsequently dissipate. However, where land titles were questionable, a small number of freed slaves actually did benefit from land allotment and legal support to secure property via the Freedmen's Bureau.

The United States Congress's intent to distribute forty acres and a mule throughout the population of freed slaves never materialized. As a result, slaves languished for many years. Most former slaves stayed on as sharecroppers with White landowners. Others sought employment in towns and villages at menial wages. Still others migrated their way north and west in search of a better existence. Essentially, millions of former slaves were set free into the vastness of America, ignorant, illiterate, and oppressed, without much more than the clothes on their back.

The following is an excerpt from the National Archives as evidence of the good intent of certain U.S. government bodies:

In the Field, Savannah, Georgia, January 16th, 1865. Special Field Orders, No. 15.

I.   The islands from Charleston, south, the abandoned rice fields along the rivers for thirty miles back from the sea, and the country bordering the St. Johns River, Florida, are reserved and set apart for the settlement of the Negroes now made free by the acts of war and the proclamation of the President of the United States.

II. At Beaufort, Hilton Head, Savannah, Fernandina, St. Augustine and Jacksonville, the Blacks may remain in their chosen or accustomed vocations—but on the islands, and in the settlements hereafter to be established, no White person whatever, unless military officers and soldiers detailed for duty, will be permitted to reside; and the sole and exclusive management of affairs will be left to the freed people themselves, subject only to the United States military authority and the acts of Congress. By the laws of war, and orders of the President of the United States, the Negro is free and must be dealt with as such. He cannot be subjected to conscription or forced military service, save by the written orders of the highest military authority of the Department, under such regulations as the President or Congress may prescribe. Domestic servants, Blacksmiths, carpenters and other mechanics, will be free to select their own work and residence, but the young and able-bodied Negroes must be encouraged to enlist as soldiers in the service of the United States, to contribute their share towards maintaining their own freedom, and securing their rights as citizens of the United States.

III. Negroes so enlisted will be organized into companies, battalions and regiments, under the orders of the United States military authorities, and will be paid, fed and clothed according to law. The bounties paid on enlistment may, with the consent of the recruit, go to assist his family and settlement in procuring agricultural implements, seed, tools, boots, clothing, and other articles necessary for their livelihood.

IV. Whenever three respectable negroes, heads of families, shall desire to settle on land, and shall have selected for that purpose an island or a locality clearly defined, within the limits above designated, the Inspector of Settlements and Plantations will himself, or by such subordinate officer as he may appoint, give them a license to settle such island or district, and afford them such assistance as he can to enable them to establish a peaceable agricultural settlement. The three parties named will subdivide the land, under the supervision of the Inspector, among themselves and such others as may choose to settle near them, so that each family shall have a plot of not more than (40) forty acres of tillable ground, and when it borders on some water channel, with not more than 800 feet water front, in the possession of which land the military authorities will afford them protection, until such time as they can protect themselves, or until Congress shall regulate their title. The Quartermaster may, on the requisition of the Inspector of Settlements and Plantations, place at the disposal of the Inspector, one or more of the captured steamers, to ply between the settlements and one or more of the commercial points heretofore named in orders, to afford the settlers the opportunity to supply their necessary wants, and to sell the products of their land and labor.

V. Whenever a negro has enlisted in the military service of the United States, he may locate his family in any one of the settlements at pleasure, and acquire a homestead, and all other rights and privileges of a settler, as though present in person. In like manner, Negroes may settle their families and engage on board the gunboats, or in fishing, or in the navigation of the inland waters, without losing any claim to land or other advantages derived from this system. But no one, unless an actual settler as above defined, or unless absent on Government service, will be entitled to claim any right to land or property in any settlement by virtue of these orders.

VI. In order to carry out this system of settlement, a general officer will be detailed as Inspector of Settlements and Plantations, whose duty it shall be to visit the settlements, to regulate their police and general management, and who will furnish personally to each head of a family, subject to the approval of the President of the United States, a possessory title in writing, giving as near as possible the description of boundaries; and who shall adjust all claims or conflicts that may arise under the same, subject to the like approval, treating such titles altogether as possessory. The

same general officer will also be charged with the enlistment
and organization of the negro recruits, and protecting their
interests while absent from their settlements; and will be
governed by the rules and regulations prescribed by the
War Department for such purposes.

VII.Brigadier General R. Saxton is hereby appointed Inspector of
Settlements and Plantations, and will at once enter on the
performance of his duties. No change is intended or desired
in the settlement now on Beaufort [Port Royal] Island, nor
will any rights to property heretofore acquired be affected
thereby.

By Order of Major General W. T. Sherman
Special Field Orders, No. 15, Headquarters Military Division of the
Mississippi, 16 Jan. 1865. Orders and Circulars, ser. 44, Adjutant
General's Office, Record Group 94, National Archives.

This order was responded to by the first session assembly of
the Thirty-ninth Congress in January of 1866, where the House
of Representatives elected to amend Senate Bill No. 60, with an
act to enlarge the powers of the Freedmen's Bureau to continue
provisions of the above order and extend it to freedmen in all parts
of the United States. After the assassination of President Abraham
Lincoln, his successor, Andrew Johnson, revoked Sherman's orders,
and the statute introduced as U.S. Senate Bill No. 60 made no
mention of grants of land or mules, which consequently subverted
what could have been an enormous economical foundation by
which recently freed slaves could begin to substantially participate
in America's capitalistic system.

While the proposal of forty acres and a mule was never
an official legislative enactment, there were times when it
appeared that legislation would pass to help freed slaves become
economically independent from their role as sharecroppers for their
former masters. Unfortunately, because of decreasing legislative
oversight of Northern Whites and increasing legislative opposition
by Southern Whites, no legislation was upheld, passed, and
enacted that would specifically help the former slaves acquire

property and improve their economic position as they transitioned from slavery to freedom.

Other missed opportunities to enrich African Americans with land rights occurred with the passage of Homestead legislation. In 1862, President Abraham Lincoln signed the landmark legislation called the Homestead Act. The act's passage was made possible by the secession of Southern states from the Union, which removed the slavery issue. The new law established a three-step process for acquiring homestead land:

1. File an application
2. Improve the land
3. File for deed of title

Any U.S. citizen of at least twenty-one years of age, who had never fought against the U.S. government, could file an application to claim 160 acres of government land. Over the next five years, the homesteader had to live on the land, build a twelve-by-fourteen-foot shelter, and grow crops. After five years, the homesteader could file for his deed of title by submitting proof of residency and the required improvements to the federal land office. After the case was filed and examined, the claimant was granted interest in the land free and clear, after a small registration fee was paid.

By 1934, over 1.5 million homestead applications were processed and more than 245 million acres, 10 percent of all U.S. lands passed from the U.S. government into the hands of individuals, very few Black.

When the Homestead Act of 1862 first passed, the country was on the brink of Civil War. It is interesting to note the impact of the legislation on the 4.5 million Blacks who were at the time slaves, but would soon become free.

Most Blacks could not acquire public land prior to the Civil War because they were not considered citizens. After the end of the Civil War and the introduction of the Emancipation Proclamation, the situation for free Black men and women depended on local circumstances. In 1865, White Southerners put obstacles in place to prevent ex-slaves from acquiring property, prevented Black landownership, and enacted measures of social control that, as a practical matter, instituted a new form of slavery. The Freedmen's Bureau invalidated such acts against Blacks, but without strong federal support and enforcement of the Freedmen's Bureau policies and practices, opposition to Black land ownership made acquiring property very difficult for freed slaves.

Ironically, Black men, many ex-slaves, who fought for the Union Army during the Civil War and later served as Buffalo Soldiers[8] to help protect settlers on the frontier from outlaws and Indian attacks were also denied the opportunity to make land claims in areas where they diligently fought and served.

In 1866, Congress passed the Southern Homestead Act where forty-six million acres of public land in Alabama, Arkansas, Florida, Louisiana, and Mississippi were set aside for purchase in 80- and 160-acre plots. The primary beneficiaries during the first six months were to be freed slaves, which represented a rare attempt to accommodate former slaves. Unfortunately, most of the quality land had been claimed before the Civil War. What remained was primarily swampland that would have required much capital to improve the land for agricultural purposes. Before much of the land was distributed, the Southern Homestead Act, like most Reconstruction programs, was repealed.

Likewise, deliberations of the Thirty-eighth Congress in 1865 on the Freedmen's Bureau bill would have taken abandoned and confiscated lands of the South for use in forty-acre allotments by freedmen to rent and eventually own, demonstrating that there

---

8. Buffalo Soldiers were members of the U.S. Cavalry of the United States Army formed on September 21, 1866. The nickname was given to the "Negro Cavalry" by the Native American tribes they fought; the term became synonymous with all of the African American regiments formed in 1866: Ninth Cavalry Regiment; Tenth Cavalry Regiment; Twenty-fourth Infantry Regiment; Twenty-fifth Infantry Regiment.

were persons interested in granting aid and land ownership to former slaves, but the recommendations hinged upon the confiscation of large Southern plantations, which eventually lost support.

During a period where many citizens were given public land by the government, Blacks who wanted to be small farm owners had to pay for their land and struggle against obstacles that most of their White counterparts did not. This is especially unsettling given that during the initial phase of the Homestead Act, from 1863–1880, most Blacks had just been freed from slavery, faced active discrimination, and were not in a position to negotiate on equal terms.

Bypassing the Homestead Act as a vehicle to promote Black self-sufficiency and bring the freed slaves into the existing economy doing something at which they already had some experience and skill was a missed opportunity.

It is estimated that the distribution of agricultural land had, over the period from 1862 to 1938, endowed 1.6 million households with 270 million acres of land and almost completely excluded Blacks.

The outcomes of various Homestead Acts are examples of how governmental policies, economic preferences, and racial discrimination shaped the inequality of wealth between Blacks and Whites that exist to this day.

Had the United States government followed through on its moral duty to provide access to a sustainable livelihood for millions of freed slaves, the following one-hundred-plus years of land value appreciation alone would have dramatically altered the lives of generations of millions of African Americans, rendering many of their descendants far more wealthy and stable today.

If Special Field Orders, No. 15, previously described, was the only land grant targeted for freed slaves to actually be instituted legislatively, it would have rendered coastal island properties along the Carolinas, Georgian and Florida coast, the property of African Americans. Substantial land ownership in this coastal region would have dramatically altered the wealth of the African American community today. These properties include well-known destinations like Hilton Head, Savannah, and Beaufort, and would potentially have spawned a variety of Black-owned and operated resort communities, enabling Blacks to commercialize the hospitality and service skills acquired over a few hundred years.

This example represents a foundation of land wealth that if appraised in 2008 dollars, this heavily resort-oriented property would be valued at billions of dollars, changing the socioeconomic outcome of several generations of a few thousand Black families. Who knows what may have evolved from the opportunities created by these wealthy land owners.

Nevertheless, despite the lack of federal support and the backdrop of racism and illegal societal treatment, Blacks have carved out an existence in this country that is actually very surprising, when you consider that they have emerged from virtually nothing and without access to anything.

After slavery, some Blacks were able to buy and secure farmland, save for modest housing, and educate their children. If you consider the amount of land that did actually pass down through generations of Black families despite regular crooked acts that frequently robbed Blacks of their land, liberty, and life, it is clear to see that had there been a widespread allotment of forty acres and a mule after slavery, the degree of Black land ownership and prosperity today would be exponentially greater.

Land ownership and farming, over time, would have in turn provided the economic ability for Blacks to progress while positioning their children to participate in many of the other great industries that have emerged over the past 150 years: agriculture, steel, rubber, plastics, transportation (ground, air, and water), clothing, electronics, construction, food production and distribution, and financial services to name a few. It is reasonable to believe that by now, Blacks would not need government intervention for attaining economic equity, and that a proportionate percentage of Fortune 1000 companies would have been founded, owned, and operated by African Americans. And as a result, African American communities, colleges, and other institutions would be self-sustaining thriving entities capable of competing with similar organizations founded by anyone. African American's wealthier stature in modern society would have continued to foster, nurture, and perpetuate the kinds of relationships that conceive, develop, and support businesses and institutions of all kinds.

The unfortunate reality is that historical racial discrimination in the United States has severely stunted the growth of Black business and institutions since slavery. Dark skin and stigmatization has denied Blacks access to land, capital, customers, partners, services, and marketplaces. Today, the sad reality is that the top 100 Black businesses in the U.S. combined are smaller than each of nearly all of the individual companies on the Fortune 100 list.

Jim Crow

The Psychological Torture Chamber

Jim Crow[9] was a period when segregation was used as an attempt by Whites, primarily in the South, to completely separate the races in all aspects of life. The primary objective was to achieve,

---

9. Jim Crow laws were state and local laws enacted between 1876 and 1965. They mandated racial segregation in all public facilities, thereby systematizing economic, educational, and social disadvantages for blacks.

promote, and enforce White supremacy over Blacks. Jim Crow referred to a minstrel show character from the early 1800s, who was an old, illiterate, crippled, Black slave who embodied negative stereotypes that became commonly associated with Blacks.

Segregation became rampant in the South after the end of Reconstruction in 1877. During Reconstruction, immediately after the Civil War, Republican governments in Southern states were primarily run by Blacks and Northerners. These governments passed laws that opened up economic and political opportunities for freed slaves. In less than one decade after the Civil War, the Democratic Party began to control much of government in the Southern states. Southern Democrats, still harboring resentment from the war and the entitlements it staged for Blacks, wanted to reverse the advancements made by Blacks during Reconstruction. To that end, they passed local and state "Jim Crow" laws that specified certain places "For Whites Only" and others for "Colored." Blacks had to tolerate separate schools, transportation, restaurants, and parks, most of which were poorly funded and inferior in quality than to those of Whites. Over the next seventy-five years, Jim Crow signs went up to completely separate the races in every public place and event.

The Jim Crow system also disenfranchised Blacks by denying them voting rights and access to polling places. In the late 1880s and early 1900s, Southern states passed laws imposing voting requirements that obliterated Black voting, in spite of the Fifteenth Amendment to the Constitution of the United States, which was designed to protect the voting rights of freed slaves. These requirements included the ability to read and write, which disqualified most Blacks since they had not had access to education; the voter had to be a property owner, which few Blacks were not due to the inability to acquire land; and the voter had to pay a poll tax, which was too much money for most Blacks, who were mostly very poor. As the final obstruction to the Black vote, the polling places in the South were White only under Jim Crow.

Fundamentally, since Blacks could not vote, they were virtually powerless to prevent Whites from segregating all aspects of

Southern life. They could not prevent discrimination in public accommodations, education, economic opportunities, or housing. In addition, Blacks were frequent victims of overt racist attitudes, actions, and the hostile intent of Southern White society, who had been bitterly defeated in the Civil War and was determined to keep newly freed Blacks "in their place."

With Jim Crow, Blacks lived their lives in fear under extremely volatile and oppressive circumstances, where Blacks had no social, political, or economical advantage, and little or no support, protection, or justice from U.S. state and local governments. Finally, the will of Blacks to struggle for equality with Whites was undermined by the pervasive display of Jim Crow signage, which was a constant reminder to Blacks of their inferior status in Southern society.

Jim Crow was a government-imposed systematic form of psychological warfare that severely damaged the Black psyche in the United States for many generations, and whose effects are still felt. It perpetuated a sense of inferiority in Blacks and superiority in Whites based solely on skin color for over a hundred years after slavery ended. The pervasive White-superiority Black-inferiority belief system promoted by Jim Crow, and the prejudicial culture that ingrained psychologically throughout society and the nation, likely impacts how Americans view themselves and each other today. For it is difficult to change within one or two generations the belief that a people who have, for hundreds of years, been classified together with oxen and mules are now suddenly your equal. Likewise, it is difficult for a people oppressed for hundreds of years to suddenly possess the same feelings of entitlement as their oppressors.

One hundred years of Jim Crow compounded the damage caused to African Americans from 350 years of slavery. During slavery, you were clear about your involuntary status and place in life which you can effectively decide to accept or reject, albeit rejecting it could prove fatal. With Jim Crow, the boundaries were not always clear. The common rule can only be described as deference to White people. In the decades following slavery, the lines were not nearly as neatly drawn as during slavery. For a Southern Black who is a free American citizen, every public scenario where Whites are encountered presented a complex array of decision making and behavior displays. This preoccupation of "staying in your place" was an extremely taxing burden on the consciousness and subconscious of African Americans.

Southern Blacks particularly continued to train their children to project inferior displays of intellect, speech, and actions to avoid provoking the sensitivities of White Americans, which could subsequently cause harm or even death to the Black youngster who appeared to be "out of his place." Once again, the African American culture today is infested with survival tactics that have themselves become self-destructive traits within the African American community, as many of these survival tactics evolved into habitual and self-limiting behavior patterns characteristic of many African Americans.

Negative Black stereotypes before, during and after Jim Crow, set the stage for an all-out attack on the image of "the Black man" that the United States has only marginally begun to acknowledge, let alone rectify. During Jim Crow and for decades following, the Black man became the United States public enemy number 1. The media, the justice system, employers of all industries, and society in general treated the Black man like a plague. Blacks themselves, powerless to make any significant impact on their social image, suffered the most disabling assault of all due to the substantial loss of the talent potential of the Black male, who had been generally rejected by society, targeted, incarcerated, and set upon a downward trend of hopelessness without substantial means for economic, social, or political revival.

Lynching

Domestic Terrorism

We (Americans) have never really come to grips with this phenomenon called Lynching in America, and yet it is something that is as American as Apple Pie.
          —Gode Davis, Lynching expert and historian

Terrorism is normally a strategy used to upset the established order of society or government, and its aim is to create disruptions that would either prevent or result in the dismantling of a perceived social or political order. However, terrorism is not necessarily an instrument of insurgency. Terrorism has also been a tool of the state used to maintain the status quo of the prevailing social order. The lynching of African Americans between the period of 1865 and 1965 was a form of this type of terrorism and was tolerated by the United States government.

Lynching is punishment carried out by a mob, usually by hanging or burning, in order to intimidate, control, or manipulate a population of people. Lynchings have been more frequent in times of social and economic unrest and were the means by which the politically dominant population oppressed social challenges.

This chapter is by far the most vivid portrayal of evidence that substantiates how the United States of America infused dysfunction in its African American citizens. Any reasonable and fair-minded person exposed to the facts and images surrounding the wholesale lynching of African Americans, for nearly one hundred years, without any meaningful reaction from the U.S. government should have a consciousness awakening because this is truly disturbing history. It becomes equally disturbing when you realize the complicity in America's White society. This complicity enabled and allowed to perpetuate a social and cultural norm in local communities that supported, condoned, or ignored the violent lynching of its African American neighbors.

As a practical matter, the postslavery lynching of African Americans was worse than the murders committed against Blacks during slavery. During slavery, anyone violent toward a slave had to answer to that slave's master, as they would be disturbing another man's property, and laws were in place to protect a man's property. However, after the Civil War and during Reconstruction, there were no enforced restraints to dissuade an angry White man from violently attacking a freed slave or raping freed slave women and girls.

Lynching in the United States against African Americans, especially in the South, rose in the aftermath of the Civil War after slavery had been abolished and recently freed Black men were given the right to vote. However, lynchings by self-appointed mobs regularly took place in the United States before and after the American Civil War, from Southern states, to Western frontier settlements and Northern territories.

After the Civil war, Southern Whites initially struggled to maintain social dominance. Vigilante groups such as the Ku Klux Klan (KKK) initiated extrajudicial assaults and lynchings to keep power and to discourage the freed slaves from voting, working, or pursuing education. The vigilante mobs would also attack teachers and agents of the Freedmen's Bureau who aided the freed slave's progress.

The aftermath of the Civil War was a period of disorder and social turmoil, and most lynch mobs consisted of Southern White men who were angry war veterans. The lynch mobs usually alleged various crimes for which they lynched Blacks. However, many Blacks were lynched for simply being successful entrepreneurs or for achieving certain levels of educational accomplishment.

In the late nineteenth century, journalist Ida B. Wells proved that many of the crimes that lynched Blacks were alleged to have committed, were exaggerated, or did not occur at all.

The sentiment and ideology behind lynching was directly linked to the political and social inequality of the time, which was precisely summarized by Benjamin Tillman,[10] the governor of South Carolina and future United States senator, who said, "We of the South have never recognized the right of the Negro to govern White men, and we never will. We have never believed him to be the equal of the White man, and we will not submit to his gratifying his lust on our wives and daughters without lynching him." These are the beliefs and

---

[10] Benjamin Ryan Tillman, an openly racist Democrat, served as the eighty-fourth governor of South Carolina, from 1890 to 1894, and as a United States senator from 1895 until his death.

words of a prominent figure of U.S. state and federal legislatures and were shared by many government officials of the time, particularly in the South.

According to Tuskegee University, which is recognized as the official expert on documented lynchings, there were 4,743 lynchings by White citizens in the United States between 1882 and 1968. While some of the offenders were the "lynch mob," many others witnessed the lynchings and even rejoiced in the events. However, Tuskegee University's numbers do not include lynchings that occurred before and during the Civil War, or lynchings immediately after the Civil War during the Reconstruction period when race relations, particularly in the South, were at their worst. In addition, Tuskegee's criteria for a murder to be documented as a lynching statistic required that there be at least three people in the lynch mob. Emmett Till, the fifteen-year-old Chicago boy who was lynched by two Mississippi White men in 1955, is a clear case where this criterion underestimates the true number of lynched Black men.

It is estimated that as many as ten thousand African Americans have been killed in the history of the United States, including lynching (documented and undocumented), random hate crimes, riots, and massacres.[11] And until recently, no Whites were ever fully prosecuted, convicted, and sentenced for coordinating, initiating, and executing these acts.

A more recent lynching occurred in Jasper, Texas, in 1998 when James Byrd, a forty-nine-year-old African American man was dragged to death behind a pickup truck driven by Shawn Berry and including Lawrence Brewer and John King. Berry was convicted and sentenced to life in prison while Brewer and King were convicted to death behind this modern-day lynching. This case demonstrates justice in modern times where White men are

---

[11] The Tulsa Race War was a massacre of mainly Blacks during a large civil disorder confined mainly to the racially segregated Greenwood neighborhood of Tulsa, Oklahoma, USA, on May 31, 1921. The Red Cross estimated three hundred dead, grave diggers estimated at three thousand.

appropriately punished for killing a Black man, albeit too late for the past mutilation of thousands of Blacks.

The following table classifies documented lynchings by the alleged cause of the lynching:

Causes of Lynchings, 1882-1968	Number	%
Homicides	1,937	40.82
Felonious Assault	205	4.32
Rape	912	19.22
Attempted Rape	288	6.09
Robbery and Theft	232	4.89
Insult to a White Person	85	1.81
All Other Causes	1,084	22.85
Total	4,743	100.00
Source: Statisics from the Archives at Tuskegee Institute		

The scale of these documented lynchings in the United States equates to, on average, at least one Black man, woman, child, or some combination, was murdered every week, between 1882 and 1968 by a hate-driven White mob. Keep in mind that there were potentially thousands of undocumented lynchings, as well as miscellaneous murders resulting from ordinary individual or mob action events.

Members of the lynch mobs often took photographs of their accomplishment to spread awareness and fear of their power. Some of those photographs were published and sold as postcards in the early twenty-first century, which further demonstrates the U.S. government's lack of reaction to this cruel activity against Blacks, as the U.S. Postal Service aided in the delivery of these shameful artifacts.

James Allen, a lynching artifact collector, published his collection of lynching photos in book form and online, with written words and a video presentation of the images. James

Allen's presentation can be found on his Web site at the following address: www.withoutsanctuary.org.

For over one hundred years in communities all across the United States of America, thousands of Black people would be killed publicly, with thousands of people witnessing, and no one would ever be convicted. Imagine what this has done to the psyche of African American people, when you know this complicity exists within the legal system to basically sanction the public murder of Blacks?

How do African Americans relate to a governmental authority that does not care about them? How do Black men relate to spouses and children with whom they are powerless to protect? How do African Americans relate to their White neighbors around whom they have to watch every word they say, every physical gesture they make, and every interaction public or private?

The experience of uncontested lynching is so traumatic that it alone is enough to sap the will and ambition out of Black people, let alone the general environment of racism and oppression. This was the ever-present reality and experience for African Americans for over one hundred years after slavery was abolished.

Without an acknowledgment or apology, or some effort to repair or reprimand the effect of lynching, it became very difficult for African Americans to trust a government and institutions that have refused to confront this history.

Recently, people have asked, "Should we prosecute old men who have been involved in these atrocities?" The answer is a resounding yes. The fact that we failed to prosecute and convict these old men when they were young men is no reason to allow justice to be forsaken. Most of these men, if not already dead, have been permitted to live their most productive years in freedom, instead of in prison. Failure to prosecute and convict these men during their terrorist rampage has been a failure of the rule of law, and the victims were not just the ones killed, but their families and the African American community at large and the integrity of what America stands for. These aging perpetrators of crimes against humanity should have been pursued, sifted out, and brought to justice just as the old Nazi regime members are who participated in the Holocaust against Jews.

The following photos are representative of many similar photos that document the horror of lynching, the disregard for African American life and human dignity, the communal participation and endorsement of the White community, and the senseless pain and suffering inflicted upon African American families.

Marion, Indiana, 1930; two young African American men are lynched in the public square.

Location unknown; late nineteenth or early twentieth century; a crowd of Caucasian men surround two African American men hanging from nooses on a pole, and one laying on the ground.

St. Joseph Missouri, 1933; a crowd stormed the Buchanan County Jail and removed Lloyd Warner, an African American accused of attacking a white woman, strung him up to a tree, and then burned his body with gasoline.

Fort Lauderdale, Florida, 1935; a crowd gathers to view the body of 32-year-old Rubin Stacy hanging from a tree. Stacy was lynched by masked men who seized him from sheriff's deputies for allegedly attacking a White woman.

While there are hundreds of photos documenting lynchings and identifying perpetrators and witnesses, most lynching atrocities were not photographed, and the perpetrators of these heinous acts of violence were rarely, if ever, held accountable for their crimes. Furthermore, African American families were left in grief and mourning, without any restitution for the loss of a husband, father, brother or son, which also had an economic impact on the family.

Segregation

Reinforced Second-Class Status

Throughout the wonderful history of the building of America, African Americans, due primarily to their inability to "blend in," faced extreme obstacles and prejudices not encountered by Whites. Blacks were barred from most educational institutions, limited to the least desirable residential and farming areas, prohibited from practicing trades and opening businesses, and generally segregated in public and private institutions, organizations, and places of worship.

In most states, Black voting was restricted, and in many Northern states, especially in the Midwest, Blacks could not serve on juries or testify against Whites in court. Blacks were prohibited from migrating to Indiana, Michigan, Wisconsin, and Iowa, and Illinois threatened bondage for Blacks who attempted to locate there permanently.

For hundreds of years, during a period where the greatest country in the world was taking shape, free Blacks were marginalized and controlled, had limited access to resources, and lived under constant threat. In addition, African American's job opportunities were always restricted, and education and poverty were continual problems.

After slavery, most free Black men worked as sharecroppers or field hands. As Blacks moved from the plantations, many worked as servants or as day laborers finding temporary work where they could. Still others worked as porters on passenger trains, sailors aboard trading ships, or laborers on loading docks. Black women most often worked as maids, laundresses, or cooks in homes, hotels, restaurants, or other businesses. Nearly all worked on the bottom rungs of the economic ladder throughout their entire adult lives.

In the South, segregation was legally enforced and generally separated the races in all areas of life. Segregation reinforced "White superiority" and "Black inferiority" in very direct ways. Whites could freely access facilities, goods, and services regardless of the level of sophistication or crudeness represented by the establishment pursued. Blacks, on the other hand, were restricted from the mainstream regardless of their character, behavior, class, or income. Blacks could not eat in most restaurants or stay at hotels of their choosing. In addition, in organizations that would cater to Blacks and Whites, Blacks were relegated to the most undesirable accommodations, i.e., the back of the bus, the basement apartment, the maintenance crew in restaurants and hotels, the porter on trains, baggage handlers, garbage handlers, and the like. Segregation attempted to control every aspect of Black life from employment, transportation, voting, and education, to housing, politics, and interracial marriage.

Although legal segregation was abolished by 1968, the lack of strong government intervention enabled segregation to remain prevalent in most Northern and Southern cities. In the 1960s and 1970s, you could still find remnants of this era if you were unfortunate enough. I remember being a ten-year-old boy traveling to Cairo, Illinois, where my mother is from, and going to a store where I attempted to sit on a bar stool. My cousin, who was ten years my senior, swiftly corrected my inappropriate action and made it clear that I could not sit while he bought goods. This was 103 years after the Emancipation Proclamation.

Blacks tended to live in all-Black neighborhoods, often called ghettos with some being characterized as slums. The formation of Black ghettos primarily resulted from real estate agents, banks, and city zoning decisions that dictated housing patterns. Often, real estate agents would not show Blacks homes in White neighborhoods while banks refused to loan money to Blacks moving into White neighborhoods. Conversely, real estate agents would create panic in White neighborhoods where Blacks have moved in, creating an opportunistic exodus of Whites.

City planners often kept neighborhoods segregated through decisions on where to locate public housing, interstate highways, access ramps to those highways, and even subway and train stations. This was quite apparent in the 1980s as you travel the highways through American cities often passing large concrete public housing relics on one side, separated by the highway from architectural normalcy on the other.

While legal segregation in schools disappeared, school officials often designed school district boundaries aimed at keeping Blacks and Whites separated. In addition, suburbanization increased segregation as Whites increasingly left the cities for suburban communities rather than live near Blacks, or have their children attend schools with Blacks.

The practice of segregation is one of the most powerful disablers of African American people in the United States of America. Segregation enabled the perpetual state of prejudice to exist, which occurs when you are simply different and separated from other people. The continuation of stereotypical beliefs is reinforced since exposure into the lives of the other people is only through mass media. Unfortunately, for decades, mass media presented African Americans, particularly Black men, in a negative light.

The bombardment of negative images of Blacks in print, and into the living rooms of White America through television, went uncontested for most Whites since most Whites were not exposed to Blacks enough to form a critical analysis against the stereotypical images presented by mass media, which formed their perceptions. As a result, the promotion of second-class citizenry of Blacks in the American society seemed natural because of the obvious lack of social and cultural assimilation of Blacks. Ironically, the lack of social and cultural assimilation by Blacks can be largely attributed to conditions imposed upon Blacks and persisted within the Black community. Additionally, once communities became completely Black and the economic blood of the community waned, the community, in many instances, became socioeconomically deprived and often filled its inhabitants with despair.

The lack of diversity left the Black communities void of exposure to critical societal roles and functions where Blacks continue to be underrepresented. Blacks have historically been left out of the economic engine in the United States. Critical knowledge and information, which can only be gained from close observation, is a missing ingredient in far too many Black lives. Many Blacks have no exposure to "White collar" high-professional careers such as doctors, lawyers, accountants, bankers, etc. In addition, know-how associated with producing the goods and services consumed by America became limited since many companies across many industry sectors fled the communities where Blacks live. Not only had these companies provided jobs within the boundaries of these neighborhoods, but they also provided insight into their operations for those employees who might have been ambitious enough to launch their own enterprise.

Segregation denied many Black Americans the opportunity to become better integrated into the American mainstream and culture and assimilate many of the activities that contribute to social and economic success. While education, desire, and ambition are important ingredients for success in America, there is no replacement for the value that comes from a network of relationships with powerful, influential, and well-connected people who favor you. Through these important relationships, visibility and possibilities emerge. These relationships support and promote an individual's upward mobility and access to future opportunities. This is what is sorely missing from the Black community. The possibility for value and exposure from trusted influential interracial connections were stripped from Blacks as a result of segregation.

Segregation dramatically reduced the probability that many Whites would become less Black phobic, and that many Blacks could learn to swim in the mainstream as a result of their direct access to the many cultural and occupational activities of their White brethren. Consequently, predominantly Black communities continued to suffer from the lingering ramifications of oppression in America: poor access to jobs, capital, education, and community services.

Economic deprivation and little access to jobs greatly compounded segregation-related problems in the Black community. Discrimination in hiring meant that Blacks held primarily low-level jobs and earned less than Whites at any job level, and as a result, Blacks had less money for housing and associated goods and services. Even where Blacks had access to better housing, in integrated neighborhoods, most could not afford to move there as Blacks generally earn less. Also, many Blacks chose to live in neighborhoods with other Blacks, just as Whites chose to live with other Whites.

Blacks who chose to integrate neighborhoods often faced violence and intimidation and would often return to inferior housing in predominantly Black neighborhoods where the average resident is of a lower socioeconomic level than themselves. However, it would be more comfortable to live in an environment that may be beneath your means, then to risk the safety of your family in an environment where racist fear mongers would harass and intimidate you with very little or no repercussion to themselves.

Since students traditionally attend schools in the neighborhoods where they live, most city schools remained segregated. Consistent with older generally run-down and now economically bankrupt Black neighborhoods, the schools were also inferior to those of the often newer, well-funded economically stable White communities. Also, as the Black community deteriorated property values decreased, which eroded the tax base, which consequently made less and less money available to the schools.

Education, or lack thereof, has a direct link to job discrimination. Blacks generally have an inferior educational environment and have fewer educational opportunities than Whites and thus are less able to compete in the job market. When you compound the lack of quality education, with the dysfunctional dynamics that emerge in financially strained families where proper care and upkeep of property and self suffers, added to Ebonics and generally different cultural norms, all you need is a little racist predisposition based on ill-perceived stereotypes, and you get widespread job discrimination against Blacks.

These realities create despair that saps hope, further deteriorates neighborhoods, assassinates self-respect, and periodically causes urban upheaval and riots. Most Black riots result from frustration on the part of its youth, who see little or no chance of participating in the American mainstream, which constantly touts its high society and good life through every form of mass media, and inundates the minds of these abandoned people on a daily basis.

Disparity is clear even to the most uneducated of Black people as they are exposed to the "outside world" primarily through television. Today, in comparison with White Americans, Blacks have significantly more poverty, are less healthy[12] and more obese, have less access to quality healthcare, live shorter lives, are killed more often, experience more police brutality, which is often fatal, are substantially more unemployed, are substantially more incarcerated, have higher rates of infant mortality, and are much less likely to graduate high school or go to college.

---

[12] According to the *American Journal of Public Health*, Vol. 86, Issue 10 1401–1405, Black children are more likely to be in poorer health than White children.

Blacks in War

Unappreciated Patriotism

Since the formation of America, Blacks have loyally, selflessly, and reverently committed life and limb in support of American ideals, even though there was not much gain, and usually suffering in it for them. Even during the colonial period, Blacks helped Whites fight against British injustices. Blacks and Whites rioted against the Stamp Act of 1765 and other regulations imposed on the colonies before the colonies won their independence. In 1770, Crispus Attucks, a fugitive slave, led an interracial crowd of men in attacking the British guard at Boston's customs office. The soldiers fired into the crowd, killing Attucks and four others.

In 1775, when the American Revolution began, nearly all of the African Americans in North America were slaves. Most Blacks were inspired by American proclamations of freedom, and both slaves and free Blacks helped fight the British in pursuit of this illusive status. The Black minutemen at the Battle of Lexington in 1775 were among those wounded in what was the first battle of the war. African Americans also served in the Battle of Bunker Hill, where former slave Salem Poor received official commendation as "a brave and gallant soldier."

While General George Washington initially refused to recruit Black troops, the British readily enlisted Blacks, and in November 1775, Lord Dunmore, the British colonial governor of Virginia, issued a proclamation that all slaves would be received into the British forces and freed for their services.

Tens of thousands of slaves escaped from Southern plantations during this period. While some chose to fight for the British, approximately ten thousand[13] served the Revolutionary army in some capacity. Many slaves served in their owner's place in exchange for freedom. There were several Black regiments including the Rhode Island Regiment and the Massachusetts's Bucks of America. This period clearly divided Black Americans who, in pursuit of freedom and equality, supported whichever entity seemed to express their best interest.

The American Revolution emphasized the incompatibility of slavery in a free land. The injustices the colonies endured from

---

[13] According to the PBS program *Africans in American II: Revolution*, an estimated one hundred thousand African Americans escaped, died, or were killed during the American Revolution.

Britain indirectly paralleled the injustices Blacks were receiving from White America. Slaves petitioned for their freedom using the words of the Declaration of Independence. African Americans hoped that the enlightened men who wrote the words "all men are created equal" would realize the wrongness of the continued enslavement of Black Americans. Unfortunately, the success of the American Revolution promoted slavery to new heights as the new independent government allowed the slave trade to continue until 1808. In addition, under the new government, slavery became the economic anchor of the United States of America and grew exponentially in the South. Blacks had aided the perpetuation of slavery for future generations of African Americans.

During the American Civil War (1861–1865), Blacks working as slaves on plantations in the Southern United States produced the food and supplies that sustained the Confederate army. Some slaves were forced to serve the Confederate army more directly as aids to their masters turned soldier or as general lackeys and field hands. In the North, freed and escaped slaves served diligently in the Union army in hope of broader freedoms for all Blacks. By the end of the war, 179,000 Black soldiers had fought in the Civil War (10 percent of the Union army) and 19,000 in the navy.[14] Many more served their masters in the Confederacy.

> Once let the black man get upon his person the brass letter,
> U.S., let him get an eagle on his button, and a musket on his
> shoulder and bullets in his pocket, there is no power on earth
> that can deny that he has earned the right to citizenship.
> —Frederick Douglass

During World War I, military needs absorbed manpower from Northern cities enticing Black migration to urban industrial centers. Thousands of Blacks worked in industries that produced goods for the war effort. Approximately 380,000 African American men joined

---

[14.] Source: http://www.archives.gov/education/lessons/Black Soldiers in the Civil War

the U.S. armed forces and went to war.[15] About 200,000 went to Europe, and most were stationed in France and served as cooks, munitions support, laborers, and cargo handlers. Some Black regiments also saw intense combat duty and were recognized for their achievements and dedicated service by the French government.

Despite their unquestionable displays of loyalty to the United States, demonstrated military proficiency, and documented acts of bravery, Black soldiers were routinely insulted and harassed by White soldiers. American military officials even attempted to establish the Jim Crow system in France. General John Pershing issued a document called "Secret Information Concerning the Black American Troops" warning the French against treating Black soldiers as equals. The following is an excerpt from the document:

> We must prevent the rise of any pronounced degree of intimacy between French officers and Black officers. We may be courteous and amiable with the last but we cannot deal with them on the same plane as white American officers without deeply wounding the latter. We must not eat with them, must not shake hands with them, seek to talk to them or to meet with them outside the requirements of military service. We must not commend too highly these troops, especially in front of white Americans. Make a point of keeping the native cantonment from spoiling the Negro. *White Americans become very incensed at any particular expression of intimacy between white women and black men.*[16]
> —General John J. Pershing

The French ignored the warning and continued to welcome Black soldiers as heroes, which was an honor frequently deserved. The Black soldiers who formed the 369th Infantry of the United

---

15. Source: http://www.archives.gov/education/lessons/369th-infantry/ African Americans during World War I.

16. General John J. Pershing in a secret communication concerning Black American troops to the French military stationed with the American army, August 7, 1918.

States National Guard fought so valiantly in France that many were awarded France's most prestigious Medal of Honor in a public ceremony. Even today, you can find people in France who recognize and appreciate the contributions of African Americans in France during the world wars.

When WWI ended, the United States promptly extracted the Black soldiers from France so that they could not participate in the celebration parades through the streets of Paris. The United States went out of their way to ensure that the Negro soldier was put swiftly and firmly back into his place as a second-class inferior citizen of the United States of America.

Many African American soldiers met a terrible fate upon returning to the United States where awaiting them was a general hostility toward Blacks wearing military uniforms. There are documented records and photos of Black soldiers being beaten or lynched by angry Whites because they wore military uniforms.

As African American veterans returned home after WWI, White opposition to recent gains by Black Americans intensified. In 1917, a White mob invaded a Black community in East Saint Louis, Illinois, and killed a few hundred African Americans. During the same year, the U.S. Army court-martialed a group of Black soldiers and hung thirteen without the benefit of an appeal due to a Black battalion's reaction to White harassment in Houston, Texas. Many uniformed Black soldiers were attacked and killed by Whites intending to enforce racial domination. During the Red Summer of 1919, anti-Black riots occurred across the country in cities including Longview, Texas; Washington DC; and Chicago, Illinois. Attacks against Black Americans continued into the 1920s, making life for African Americans increasingly more challenging even though slavery had ended a half century ago, and Blacks were willingly and repeatedly making the ultimate sacrifice in the country's wars.

During WWII, African Americans had to repeatedly battle adversaries on two fronts: the war enemy overseas and White racism at home. African Americans fought in World War II to ensure that the "four freedoms" would be available to others in a foreign land. The Four Freedoms were as follows:

1. Freedom of speech
2. Freedom of religion
3. Freedom from want
4. Freedom from fear

While Blacks were fighting abroad, their own families were being subjected to prejudicial practices that kept them from enjoying the "four freedoms" in the United States.

African Americans were always ready to work and fight for their country while demanding an end to discrimination against them in their homeland. Over 2.5 million African American men registered for the draft, and Black women volunteered in large numbers as well. While serving in the armed forces: army, air force, navy, Marine Corps, and Coast Guard, they could not escape discrimination and segregation. Despite this reality, many African American men and women met and exceeded the challenge before them, gaining few commendations for their sacrifices.

The Korean War was the first war to integrate Whites and Blacks in U.S. military fighting units. As White combat units began to take excessive casualties, they would normally be replaced by Whites until the launch of equality of opportunity and treatment, which commissioned Blacks, according to *Black Americans in Defense of Our Nation* written in 1991 by the Office of the Deputy Assistant Secretary of Defense for Civilian Personnel Policy and Equal Opportunity. African Americans consistently served well in Korea, proving that they could fight as well as Whites, the book notes. The Korean War was the first war since the Spanish-American War in 1898 where African Americans were credited by the United States government for their heroic contributions.

The United States presence in the Vietnam War consisted of a disproportionate number of poor and Black men who fought and died, or were injured on behalf of the United States of America. Over sixty-nine thousand men were killed and tens of thousands more were injured physically or mentally. The Vietnam War left hundreds of thousands of mothers in sorrow, tens of thousands of heartbroken wives and sweethearts, thousands of fatherless children, and tens of thousands of young men in a country that did not appreciate or respect them for the war and/or their race.

Black men in particular would return home to not only the negative war sentiment, but to ghetto communities, persistent Jim Crow conditions, racial injustice and humiliation, police brutality and an unjust justice system, few opportunities for good jobs, and a climaxing civil rights movement.

By the height of the Vietnam War, Black leaders vigorously denounced United States participation and the racist nature of the war. Dr. Martin Luther King Jr., veered from his traditional "civil rights" stand to speak out against the war. Professional boxer Muhammad Ali, when drafted, refused to join the military for religious beliefs and stated that "no Viet Kong ever called me a nigger." Many would begin to stand up to the injustices that the war represented for poor and African American citizens and the benefit gained by so few from the perpetration of the war while the African American community continued to gain so little.

African Americans have always unselfishly served in support of the United States of America even when there was strong American opposition against their service, and uniformed Blacks would be regularly spat upon, sneered, and sometimes beaten or killed as they walked the streets of America. Ironically, Black soldiers would be well treated by American allies, particularly France, where a Black soldier would not be treated differently from a White soldier under any circumstances. France openly acknowledged the unfortunate treatment of Black soldiers in the United States when they too were making the ultimate sacrifice.

Black soldiers routinely proved their loyalty and allegiance to America even though America systematically placed Blacks in politically, economically, and socially marginalized positions. While this American institutionalized negative treatment of Blacks was rampant and overt throughout the nation, with the exception of pockets of "right hearted" groups and individuals, Blacks have, for the most part, "grinned and bared it" as the reality of the times dictated since as a minority population your attempts to revolt could prove futile.

After the Civil War and Reconstruction period, segregation had swept the nation separating all aspects of White and Black life. As a result, Blacks were not fully integrated with White soldiers during WWI and WWII and were mainly relegated to supporting roles and not battlefields. However, when Black regiments were called upon to fight, their heroics and battle excellence[17] were undeniable, which caused the acceleration of Black participation in military operations for many wars to come. Unfortunately, the psyche of many African Americans festered a growing sense of hopelessness and helplessness, when realizing that the very system that is in place to support them is the primary deliverer of their pain and suffering. While Black soldiers were off diligently fighting America's external enemies sometimes in an effort to earn Black acceptance in America, Blacks at home would, at the same time, suffer the worst of what ill-hearted and misguided White Americans had to offer.

- Mental and physical abuse
- Unequal access to housing, jobs, hospitality, and transportation services
- Unequal institutional access to education, health care, and capital

This would be the reward awaiting the brave soldiers who fought and sacrificed everything for the country they loved.

The lack of strong government intervention on behalf of its Black citizens enabled a disadvantaged situation to perpetuate for decades. It helped create a permanent underclass culture in Black America, which would ironically be despised and ridiculed by White

---

[17] For example, during WWII, the Tuskegee Airmen flew over sixty missions across Europe protecting U.S. bombers and never lost a single bomber.

America, who controlled and operated all major companies and institutions with the power to accept or reject Black participation. It is like much of White America looks at Black America and wonders, "What is wrong with these people?" without any remembrance, acknowledgment and understanding of the hundreds of years of oppression that has been, and continue to be, albeit indirect, inflicted upon these loyal American citizens, which has rendered them dysfunctional and outcast members of society.

The Civil Rights Movement

Crying for Justice

In 1875, Congress passed a Civil Rights Act to bar segregation in public facilities. This government ruling was not effectively enforced in the Southern states for decades. Blacks, however, sought not integration with Whites, but freedom from White interference in their activities. A primary goal of freed slaves was to own land, but most former slaves lacked the resources to buy land, and real property remained predominately controlled by Whites. Since 1865, newly freed African Americans signed labor contracts with planters to do field work in exchange for wages, housing, food, and clothing. As a result, the labor system of sharecropping evolved. Under sharecropping, landowners rented small parcels of land to Blacks for a percentage of the crop they harvested. The former slaves soon found the new system to be very similar to slavery.

After the early civil rights enactments, for more than seventy-five years, legislation regarding civil rights for Blacks took a backseat to other issues until it became a major national political issue in the 1950s. The first federal civil rights law since Reconstruction was enacted in 1957 and authorized the U.S. attorney general to enforce voting rights. Almost a century had passed since Blacks became free American citizens.

In 1960, the civil rights laws were strengthened, and in 1964, a widespread civil rights bill outlawed racial discrimination in public institutions and private organizations including corporations. In addition, since normal judicial procedures were too slow in assuring African American registration and voting, Congress passed a voting rights bill in 1965. The law banned the use of literacy or other voter-qualification tests that kept Blacks off voting lists. Literacy restrictions had now been a primary source of Black voter deterrence in Southern states for one hundred years.

During the 1960s, demonstrators in the civil rights movement protested against segregation throughout the South and in many Northern cities across the United States. The protesters recruited like-minded individuals and held rallies, boycotted segregated institutions and businesses, rigorously registered Black voters, and frequently marched to bring an end to segregation.

Demonstrators were routinely beaten and arrested by police, and many were injured and murdered by the Ku Klux Klan (KKK) and other White terrorist organizations. At the height of the civil rights movement, two important civil rights leaders, Medgar Evers and Dr. Martin Luther King Jr. were assassinated.

In Southern states, the police regularly conspired with local members of the KKK to threaten, attack, or murder civil rights workers of any race or ethnicity. The collaboration between law enforcement authorities and White terrorist groups made civil rights activism an extremely deadly proposition only suited for the most courageous and dedicated citizens Black or White.

In response to increasing civil rights protests, the U.S. Congress passed new civil rights laws in 1964, 1965, and 1968. The Civil Rights Act of 1964 targeted racial discrimination in public education, public accommodations, and by employers or voter registrars. The Voting Rights Act of 1965 suspended the use of voter literacy tests, which were used to prevent Blacks from voting. A 1968 act was designed to outlaw racial discrimination in federally funded housing projects. This legislation was not well received or enforced by many within the institutions and businesses that represented mainstream America.

Without appropriate enforcement mechanisms to verify the compliance of the laws, particularly regarding intangibles like discrimination, people will continue to operate based on their own values, biases, and beliefs, which cannot be legislated and may not be in the best interest of the nation at large.

As a practical matter, the civil rights movement ended in 1968 with the death of Martin Luther King Jr. and the subsequent riots. Even though social gains resulted from the movement, full equality may never be achieved because African Americans are so far behind, and racial problems continued to exist in the United States long after King's assassination.

Into the 1970s and 1980s, urban poverty continued to be a growing problem and remain disproportionately high among Blacks. Well conceived and loosely executed were the affirmative-action programs, which emerged in the 1970s to support the hiring and promotion of minorities and women. These programs resulted from the backlash of the civil unrest of the 1960s but were short-lived in their intensity toward righting past wrongs toward Blacks. However, White women benefited significantly from these efforts.

During the late 1900s, Blacks made impressive gains in education, employment, and, to a lesser degree, housing. Nevertheless, historic patterns of hiring and promotion leave African Americans economically vulnerable, especially in times of a weak national economy. In 1986, the Supreme Court supported the limited use of affirmative action to help compensate African American groups for past job discrimination, and in 1987, the Court upheld the right of employers to extend preferential treatment to minorities and women in order to achieve a better balanced workforce. However, in 1989, the Court's conservative majority moved toward reversing this direction by making it even more difficult for women and minorities to use the courts to remedy discrimination in hiring practices or on the job. In response, Congress passed the Civil Rights Act of 1991, which strengthened affirmative action.

Now that the "civil smoke" has cleared, it is largely business as usual except for public organizations, those competing for government contracts, and companies sensitive to revenue exposure in African American communities. Otherwise, for most companies and institutions in America, business as usual does not readily embrace Blacks into the power structures and influential levels of corporate America. Blacks generally are not significantly ingrained in the social and professional networks that drive opportunities within organizations.

While full equality seems to be in the distant future, the civil rights movement did accomplish some fundamental reforms across America. Legal segregation as a system of racial control and divide was completely publicly dismantled, and Blacks were relieved from the public humiliation of the Jim Crow laws. Unofficially, Jim Crow continued for several years in Southern and rural areas where intimidation from local White supremist groups continued to influence Black behavior. Otherwise, public institutions everywhere were opened to everyone. More importantly, Blacks unconditionally achieved the right to vote and to experience the influence of voting power in a democracy. Voting would go a long way toward Blacks incrementally improving the quality of their lives in the United States of America.

The civil rights movement proved to be beneficial in breaking down many of the institutionalized oppressive mechanisms in American society. Its goals were largely accomplished by using mass media, which had, for decades, oppressed Blacks as a way to present to America the injustices forced onto nonviolent Black citizens who were simply trying to exercise their right to life, liberty, and the pursuit of happiness. The televised events of the civil rights movement served to awaken the consciousness of White America.

As a result of civil rights:

- Overt racial assaults can now land a White person in jail
- Blacks can take advantage of public resources anywhere in the country, with few exceptions
- In theory, Blacks can live anywhere they can afford
- Colleges and universities are open to all who qualify
- The media is more conscious of the ramifications of irresponsible and insensitive portrayals of Blacks and have taken steps to right their wrongs
- A growing number of government agencies, public institutions, and even some major corporations are now headed by Blacks

While these are notable accomplishments that we all should be proud of, we must acknowledge the fact that the majority of African Americans still languish in comparison to the mainstream of America.

The denial of civil rights to Blacks for over 125 years since slavery and the lack of access to good-paying jobs, education, and capital caused Blacks to miss out on hundreds of thousands of opportunities that otherwise would have changed the socioeconomic condition of Blacks today. This opportunity loss cannot be measured and results in Blacks being significantly absent from a cross section of multifaceted industries, including consumer products, manufacturing, financial services, health care, and others.

It is rarely acknowledged that Blacks were historically not allowed meaningful participation in any of the industries mentioned above. The result today is that generations of Blacks who could have been the descendants of founders, executives, and employees of companies across every major segment of the U.S. economy are largely the offspring of generations of economic "bottom feeders," with some exceptions of course. Ever since the house slave, there has always been lucky African Americans who seem to fare better than the rest. However, by and large the critical mass of the African American population has not been endowed with the "blessings" of the mainstream and have existed and survived in the bowels of the greatest nation to exist to date.

When immigrants arrive in the United States of America from a variety of foreign lands, it reasonably takes a generation or two before their offspring begins to achieve the American dream, if not accomplished by the first. In the case of most African Americans, generally speaking, twenty or more generations have come and gone without the next generation being lifted significantly above the socioeconomic level of the last. This stagnation was perpetuated by the lack of civil rights over a long period of time.

On a positive note, progress was clearly achieved by the civil rights movement. While not nearly on par with White America, the trends in the following table resulting from the civil rights legislation of 1964 are moving in the right direction:

Civil Rights Results	1964	2002
Black Population	21 mil	39 mil
Median income (male) inflation adjusted	$20,805	$31,966
Median inc (female) inflation adjusted	$13,085	$27,703
Poverty: % of U.S. Pop	41.8%	23.9%
HS Grads age 25+	26%	80%
Blacks in college	306,000	2.3 mil
College Grads age 25+	4%	17%
Blacks with at least a Bachelors degree	365,000 1.7%	3.6 mil 9.2%

Source: U.S. Census Bureau

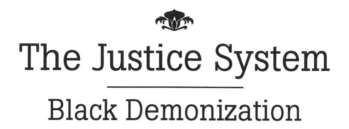

The Justice System
Black Demonization

"Your Honor, I swear I didn't do it. Police commander Burge and his men tortured me into a confession!"

The United States justice system has historically been anti-Black and has done more harm to the Black male than any other factor to date. In recent history, there is evidence of federal, state, and local law enforcement's participation in covert and oftentimes deadly activities directed against leaders in the African American community. From recorded events of the FBI spying on Dr. Martin Luther King Jr. and attempting to discredit him, to the ambush and murder of Black Panther Party members in a Chicago apartment by the Chicago Police Department, to the one and only case where a bomb was dropped on American citizens by U.S. law enforcement when a townhome in Philadelphia containing African American radicals was bombed in 1985.

The justice system within America has only recently become less hostile toward African Americans and Black men in general. In the past, Blacks experienced a system that routinely arrested Black males for crimes they had not committed, but found themselves subsequently convicted by all-White juries and imprisoned. This same system failed to convict a single White person for the thousands of Blacks regularly lynched by White mobs in the South and across the country.

African Americans are primarily targeted by law enforcement for search and seizure and, as a result, are much more frequently incarcerated for drug-related activity. The reality is that over 80 percent of all drugs are either brought into the United States or manufactured in the United States by Whites (Hispanic drug trafficking is currently reducing this percentage), and more than 80 percent of drug users are White while more than 50 percent of those incarcerated for drug activity are African American, who represent only 12 percent of the overall population. In addition, Blacks convicted of all crimes routinely receive stiffer penalties than Whites similarly convicted.[18]

[18.] According to the *Journal of Quantitative Criminology*, Vol. 21, No. 4, December 2005, African Americans generally are sentenced more harshly than Whites; the magnitude of this race effect is statistically significant but small and highly variable.

Ironically, in the first half of the twentieth century, U.S. penitentiaries housed predominately (over 80 percent) White men. This was consistent with statistical population proportions and the racial profile of the country. Over the course of the second half of the 1900s, as Blacks migrated from the South to the North and West, a strange phenomenon occurred. The penal system that had previously been populated by predominantly White males transformed into being populated by predominantly Black males. Did White men stop committing crime? Did Black men commit more crime regardless of their relatively small percentage of the population? Did society start targeting and "capturing" Black males to institutionally "control" the group?

Year	Total Inmates	# White	% White	# Minority	% Minority
1880	58,609	52,162	89	6,447	11
1900	112,760	98,101	87	14,659	13
1920	140,067	116,256	83	23,811	17
1950	264,567	203,717	77	60,850	23
1960	346,015	235,290	68	110,725	32
1970	328,021	200,093	61	127,928	39
1980	466,371	265,831	57	200,540	43
1990	1,300,000	624,000	48	676,000	52
2000	1,935,753	813,016	42	1,122,737	58
2006	2,275,000	796,260	35	1,478,750	65

Source: Bureau of Justice Statistics

Due to racial profiling, Blacks are much more vigorously targeted by law enforcement agencies even when no apparent violation exists. This is exacerbated by a predominant discriminatory mind-set possessed by many police officers who have been mostly White at the rank-and-file level and all White in the management ranks, with few exceptions. Stereotyped perceptions enabled police officers to routinely refer to Blacks as niggers, monkeys, and moolies, depending on their own national origin or ethnicity. It is very improbable to treat a human being fairly and with dignity and respect when you normally refer to them in any of the terms just mentioned. As a result, Blacks are arrested much more frequently with or without cause, and in some cases, the mere act of police harassment creates a scenario where cause can erupt or at least be alluded to by police officers. Of course, in the court of law, the word of the police as an agent of the government is more credible than that of an often economically disadvantaged Black male, particularly in the eyes of a White judge or jury.

Conversely, many Whites violate the law through drug abuse, theft of all sorts, traffic violations, and the like, with the unique privilege of minimized scrutiny due to their skin color. The reality, purely from a statistically proportioned population perspective, is that most crime is committed by Whites, including drug trafficking and/or abuse, sexual offenses, petty crime, robbery, burglary, theft, grand larceny, and white-collar crimes. The sheer volume of Whites in the United States would result in a justice system where the defendants would be at least half White, as it was before the great migration of Blacks from the South. Nearly everyone knows a White person who participates in some illegal act, particularly drug abuse. White crime is common, but the establishment is no longer watching Whites with even a fraction of the focus and scrutiny given to Blacks.

In addition to decades of racial profiling and targeting of Blacks by law enforcement, Blacks have been routinely falsely accused and consistently incarcerated for crimes they had not committed. There are several cases where a White man or woman "staged" a criminal event and reported to police that a Black male was the perpetrator. Consider these events:

- Boston, 1989, a White man, Charles Stuart, coolly plotted, shot and killed his pregnant wife, Carol, and nearly got away with it after accusing a Black man.
- Albany, New York, 1994, after spending Thanksgiving weekend with relatives in New Hampshire, Kendra Gillis, a White college freshman, told authorities at the State University of New York at Albany that she had been attacked and beaten in her dorm room by a Black man the night she returned. Ten days later, police arrested and charged her father, David Gillis, who is White.
- South Carolina, 1994, Susan Smith, a White mother, claimed that a Black man had stolen her minivan with her children inside, creating a public manhunt and sending law enforcement on a rampage harassing Black men. She later

revealed that she drowned her children by driving them into a lake while they were asleep in their baby seats.

- New York, 1989, five Black teenagers from Harlem were accused of raping a White female jogger in New York City's Central Park. The five Black men were ultimately released from prison and had their records erased after being arrested without any supporting evidence. These young men, known as the Central Park 5, were convicted even though the rape victim never saw her attackers. DNA evidence finally proved them innocent, and another man confessed to the crime.

In these fraudulent cases, Black males are quickly arrested fitting some arbitrary description that was completely imagined to begin with.

Conversely, there are several acts of crime, particularly murder, where the indications are that the perpetrator is White, and years go by without any progress on the case, let alone an arrest. And statistically speaking, there are over ten times as many potential candidates to arrest when the suspect is White. Consider these examples:

- More than ten years passed without any meaningful progress toward an arrest and conviction for the murder of six-year-old Jon Benet Ramsoy, killed in Bolder, Colorado, on Christmas Day 1996.
- Twenty-seven years passed before the Kennedy relative Michael Skakel was convicted of beating his teenage neighbor Martha Moxley to death with a golf club in 1975.
- The execution style murder of James McVey in Fort Worth, Texas, in 1994, where James's face was painted blue indicating some type of revenge, and there were bloody footprints, expended shells identifying the murder weapon, but never an arrest.
- The murder of Jimmie Sue Smith in Lubbock, Texas, where Jimmie Sue's body was found nude with a necktie around her throat, feet, and hands. Jimmie Sue's murder took place in broad daylight indicating that the killer felt comfortable

in her neighborhood, and the killer's dress, mannerisms, race, and auto would not seem out of place in an all White community.

- Robert Wone was murdered in 2006 in his friend's Washington DC apartment. He had been restrained, incapacitated, and sexually assaulted prior to his death. Wone's friends, residents of the apartment, were present at the time of the murder. They, however, claimed that an intruder committed the crime. The authorities found no evidence of a break-in, and the crime scene evidence was not consistent with the residents' statements.
- More recently, on May 7, 2009, Drew Peterson of Bolingbrook, Illinois, was finally arrested after two of his former wives were either found dead or missing. If Drew Peterson was a Black man, and White families were alleging his involvement in wrongdoing related to these young White ladies, it is extremely likely that Drew would have met a different fate in our justice system. And it would not have taken nearly seven years to accomplish.

Clearly, in each of these cases, except for the last, someone could have at least been arrested. Had there been a Black man suspected in these cases, probability is extremely high that there would have been an arrest, almost immediately.

The pattern has been that if the victim is White and the suspect is Black, then a Black person is aggressively apprehended regardless of the evidence; but when the suspect is potentially White, and no solid evidence exists, then no one is aggressively pursued.

One of our country's biggest injustice is the number of Black men incarcerated or murdered as the result of being falsely accused by Whites down through history. Some of the worst cases would include Southern scenes of a Black man being accused of rape by a White woman, resulting in the lynching of the Black man in question and significant hostility toward the local Black population in general. While not probable in every case, it stands to reason that a Black male in a racially charged and hostile environment like the South in the early 1900s, where he is clearly disadvantaged, and everyone knows everyone, would not be so bold as to rape a White woman. It also stands to reason that a sexually curious White woman would potentially lure a Black male for sexual pleasure and, if discovered, claim rape to protect her virtue, to the detriment of the Black male. This was the reality in America's South during the 1700-1900s, where in some cases Black men had to leave an entire county (i.e., Forsyth, Georgia)[19] to avoid violent treatment and hostility from the White community. The state and local governments offered little, if any, protection or support to relieve Black communities of their unfortunate victimization.

The disparity of targeting Blacks and favoring Whites is perpetuated within the processes and procedures of the justice system. In the past, district attorneys, prosecutors, and law enforcement agencies, willingly created, altered, or hid evidence when there was doubt regarding the guilt of an accused Black male. The rationale sometimes being "if he didn't commit this crime he probably committed another, so what difference does it make."

The irony is that in many cases, law enforcement and the justice system initially created a criminal out of an innocent Black man, and once convicted, a life of crime can become pre-ordained. Once you are a convicted Black male, America generally pushes you aside. Even though you have theoretically paid your debt to society, sometimes for a crime you did not commit, you are now "tagged" as a reject. The most obvious impact is your inability to secure employment. Once you check "yes" to the question "Have you ever been convicted of a crime," your chances diminish rapidly even though you're a good, hardworking person, who may have been falsely accused and convicted. You are left with few options. Even if you were actually guilty of the crime that you were convicted and served time for, society should accept you back by providing opportunities where you can become a productive

---

19. Source: http://www.pbs.org/independentlens/banished/forsyth. In the early 1900s, there were more than 1,000 African Americans in Forsyth County, Georgia, comprising 10 percent of the population. But in 1912, whites violently expelled all black residents from the county.

contributor. This of course assumes your crime was economically motivated. Instead, society creates even more obstacles and hurdles by denying certain rights and privileges that could hold the key to reform.

Since Black males are disproportionately targeted, accused, and convicted of crimes, they also carry the disproportionate burden of being marginalized and almost permanently reduced to an economically disadvantaged existence. There have been very few meaningful attempts by federal, state, and local governments to acknowledge, recognize, and begin to take steps to rectify this disparity. As a result, the Black male image and productivity continues to plummet, radiating negative habits, stereotypes, and behavior patterns throughout the core of the Black community and continually staging poor examples for Black youth to emulate.

As a result of the negative conditioning that the media and justice system has imposed on the American population, Americans consistently view Black men as criminal and Blacks in general as intellectually inferior. A Black man of any class—doctor, lawyer, businessman—is initially viewed suspiciously when first encountered. The justice system has left many Black Americans without options or hope as many of their lives have been permanently affected for oftentimes minor offenses, which regularly go unpunished in White communities. Today, over 50 percent of the men and boys incarcerated are Black while Blacks only represent 12 percent of the population.

Many Blacks who have been convicted of crimes, rightfully or not, have been forced into a subculture of criminal behavior as a means of survival. Once "outcast" from society, there are very few avenues that effectively lead to a respectable constructive existence. The negative conditioning of America is so strong that many Whites, who observed the 1991 beating of Rodney King by the LAPD after he committed a traffic violation, felt that the beating was justified. What this conditioning blinds Whites to are instances such as when in 1981, John Hinckley ambushed President Ronald Reagan's entourage shooting several people, including the president, Hinckley was only subdued and then handcuffed. Shouldn't Hinckley have at least been beaten? If anyone deserves a police beating, it is the person who tried to kill the president, not the guy who ran a red light. Obviously, Rodney king is a Black man and John Hinckley is White.

Repeatedly throughout American society today, there is substantial disparity in the way law enforcement engages with Whites versus Blacks. Even today, most Black men, even very successful men who have never had trouble with law enforcement, drive around America nervously when in the presence of a police cruiser.

Nearly all images of police brutality from beatings to shootings happen to people of color while the majority of people in the United States remain White; it's clear to see the disparity.

It is a statistical certainty that White people present more confrontational situations to law enforcement on a daily basis than do others. The privilege of White skin relieves them of the severe ramifications frequently experienced by people of color.

The worst result from decades of injustice in the justice system is that the criminalization of the Black male has become a self-fulfilled prophecy. Millions of Black men have been tainted by the system and tarnished for life relegating them to an existence that can usually only be sustained by criminal activity, leading to a pattern of incarceration. What started as racial injustice frequently applied to innocent Black men has evolved over decades of marginalization, into a culture where young Black men almost naturally gravitate toward antisocial behavior that is now common in their communities as a result of this vicious cycle and ultimately landing them in jail.

Today, the Black male is severely disproportionately overrepresented in our nation's prison system, which is a phenomenon that has occurred over the last fifty years or so. Current statistics show that more Black men go to prison each year than to college. The Black male is much more likely to be uneducated and unemployed, is highly likely to be the victim of violence or killed, is more likely to be addicted to drugs and/or alcohol, is more likely to have out-of-wedlock children, is more likely to abandon his children, is frequently involved in crime as a means of survival, and the list goes on.

The reality of the Black man today was set in motion decades earlier by an ill-intended society that regardless of innocence or guilt, targeted and unduly convicted the Black male in large enough numbers to substantially render a critical mass of Black men inept. Once you are labeled by the system, economic survival becomes a slippery slope negatively impacting your manhood, livelihood, and allowing little opportunity for future success.

According to the U.S. Department of Justice Bureau of Justice Statistics, Black males in their late twenties are incarcerated at higher rates than all other groups. At midyear 2006, more Black men (836,800) were in custody in state and federal prisons or local jails than White men (718,100) or Hispanic men (426,900) (table 1). Black men comprised 41 percent of the more than 2 million men in custody. Relative to their numbers in the general population, about 4.8 percent of all Black men (12 percent of Black men ages 25 to 29) were in custody at midyear 2006, compared to about 0.7 percent of White men and 1.9 percent of Hispanic men. Overall, Black men were incarcerated at 6.5 times the rate of White men. Across age groups, Black men were between 5.7 and 8.5 times more likely than White men to be incarcerated.

Number of inmates in State or Federal prisons and local jails, by gender, race, and age, June 30, 2006

| | Males | | | |
	Total[a]	White[b]	Black/African American[b]	Hispanic/ Latino
Total	2,042,100	718,100	836,800	426,900
18-19	75,600	24,800	33,000	15,300
20-24	365,700	111,100	160,000	84,900
25-29	359,300	103,700	156,200	90,800
30-34	328,300	109,600	132,400	78,000
35-39	298,700	110,900	120,500	58,300
40-44	262,600	107,200	103,000	43,200
45-54	257,400	105,100	101,000	41,500
55 or older	79,000	41,800	22,200	12,200

Hispanic 426,900 22%

White 718,100 36%

Black 836,800 42%

Total Prison Population: 2,042,100

Source: Bureau of Justice Statistics

Reflective of these statistics is Black male disenfranchisement. Black men are subjected to joblessness and the inability to support and maintain a household. Many with felony convictions can no longer vote or play a role in social change. While Black men are no longer routinely physically lynched, they are psychologically lynched. They are unable to adapt and cope in mainstream America in a constructive and productive capacity. They are unable to perform the primary male role accepted by cultures worldwide.

Because Black men are frequently unable to provide for their families in the traditional sense, it leads to confusion over gender roles and issues with Black women, who are forced to become the primary providers in the absence of husbands and fathers, which in turn present a challenge to the Black man's view of his masculinity.

Many Black men are already defeated due to their assumed inadequacies, which have been preconditioned by mainstream media. This prejudged inadequacy is exacerbated by the typically lower economic rung where many Black men exist, their low literacy rates, their significant high school dropout rates, and their disproportionately high unemployment rate. This state of dejection experienced by many Black men contributes to the "thug" behavior glorified by rap music. Being intellectually, socially, spiritually, and financially bankrupt, Black men generally seek to establish masculinity through various forms of community abuse and socially irresponsible behavior.

The following facts illustrate the results ultimately rendered from a historically unjust justice system:

- One in three Black men between the ages of 20 and 29 years old is under correctional supervision or control. *Source: Mauer, M. & Huling, T., Young Black Americans and the Criminal Justice System: Five Years Later (Washington DC: The Sentencing Project, 1995).*

- In 2001, the chances of going to prison were highest among Black males (32.2%) and Hispanic males (17.2%) and lowest among White males (5.9%). *Source: Bonczar, Thomas P., US Department of Justice, Bureau of Justice Statistics, "Prevalence of Imprisonment in the US Population,1974-2001," NCJ197976 (Washington DC: US Department of Justice, August 2003), p. 8.*
- Blacks account for only 12% of the U.S. population but 44% of all prisoners in the United States are Black. *Human Rights Watch*
- The rate of drug admissions to state prison for Black men is thirteen times greater than the rate for White men. A recent report by Human Rights Watch found that while drug use is consistent across all racial groups, Blacks and Latinos are far more likely to be arrested and prosecuted and given long sentences for drug offenses. Blacks constitute 13% of all drug users, but 35% of those arrested for drug possession, 55% of persons convicted, and 74% of people sent to prison. http://www.drugpolicy.org/communities/race/criminaljust/"
- Of Black males born in 2005, 29% can expect to spend some time behind bars. One in 14 Black children has a parent in jail or prison. One in 20 Black men is incarcerated, compared with one in 155 White men. For every three Black men in college, four are in prison. *Department of Justice, Bureau of Justice Statistics, "Prison and Jail Inmates at Midyear 2002," April 6, 2003.*
- In at least fifteen states, Black men were sent to prison on drug charges at rates ranging from twenty to fifty-seven times those of White men.
- Blacks are incarcerated at a rate that is more than six times that of Whites.
- Black men who had dropped out of school had spent time in prison. In the inner cities, more than half of all Black men do not finish high school.
- More young Black men in the United States have done time in prison than have served in the military or earned a college degree.

- The paper, appearing in the American Sociological Review, estimates that 20% of all Black men born from 1965 through 1969 had served time in prison by the time they reached their early 30s. By comparison, less than 3% of White males born in the same time period had been in prison. *The New York Times, http://www.nytimes.com/2006/03/20/ national/20blackmen." "Plight Deepens for Black Men, Studies Warn.", March 20, 2006*

White Flight

Reckless Abandonment

As Blacks migrated from the South to the North in search of jobs, respect, equality, and, in general, a better life, they normally found themselves landing in some of the most undesirable areas of Northern cities. This was in many cases designed by the governments of Northern cities who, while not as overtly racist as their Southern counterparts, were equally unjust in the administration of fairness and equality when it came to sharing socioeconomic resources with their fellow Black citizens.

Black neighborhoods were typically the areas of the city that were aging and previously inhabited by Whites. During the 1960s, 1970s, and 1980s, Blacks were met with extreme resistance as they attempted to move out of these inferior neighborhoods and into better environments normally occupied by Whites. In cities like Chicago, a Black who moved into the wrong White neighborhood would have placed his/her family in harm's way and was sometimes subjected to injury or death and almost always with threats or property damage. By the mid 1900s, most city governments found this treatment of Black citizens to be unacceptable, but did very little to discourage the harassment of Black citizens and often not enough to identify and prosecute the White perpetrators.

As Blacks began to gain entry into city neighborhoods where less extreme reactions could be anticipated, White flight would ensue shortly thereafter. White flight was an interesting phenomenon. It was generally ignited out of pure racist views where Whites simply did not want to live near Blacks, or it resulted from the fear of a declining neighborhood either in property valuations or in safety. The fear was fueled by unscrupulous real estate brokers who seized the opportunity to enrich themselves at the wholesale exploitation of White homeowners who bought into the perception that if Blacks moved in, "there goes the neighborhood." In fact, the first Blacks who integrated a White neighborhood were typically among the more successful Blacks in the country and oftentimes were socioeconomically superior to the Whites residing in the neighborhood the Black wished to enter. In some communities, for example the South Shore neighborhood on the south side of Chicago, where I grew up, White flight occurred so rapidly that a community of approximately fifty thousand would turn from White to Black in less than five years. This would have devastating long-term effects on the community.

First, as White flight ensued, property values trended downward as Whites became more and more desperate to flee the area and sold cheaper and cheaper. Declining property values would, in effect, enable more and more individuals of lower-income standards to now gain access to an area for which they recently could not afford. And in many of these cases, the individuals could barely buy the home, let alone properly maintain their property, and contribute to community affairs.

Secondly, as Whites left the community, the local employee pool also turned from White to Black, and the hundreds of neighborhood-based businesses found themselves in the undesirable position of employing a disproportionate number of Blacks in their operation. Most White business owners followed White homeowners and left the communities where they had operated for years. As businesses left, jobs also left the community, leaving a now predominately Black community economically bankrupt with the exception of the low capital-intensive businesses that Blacks were able to establish. Jobs and investment capital became scarcer in Black communities, causing gradual economic decay. The business fabric of the inner cities went from light industrial, manufacturing, and distribution to predominately storefront operations offering food, liquor, dry cleaning, religious services, and a variety of other microbusinesses. Clearly the economic muscle of the communities was severely weakened.

Thirdly, White flight of the '60s and '70s detrimentally impacted the generation of Blacks and Whites coming of age during this period. It became consciously and unconsciously perceived by White children forced to leave their neighborhood, school, and friends that something was terribly wrong with their new neighbors. Most children in functional family relationships hold their parents in high esteem. The decision of these parents in the eyes of their children must have been founded on credible and substantial reasoning. Whether the children wanted to move or not was irrelevant, in either case, they likely formed very negative lasting impressions regarding Black people. These impressions potentially stained their perceptions for years, as they grew up and moved on into the world to help manage the businesses and institutions of the United States of America. Conversely, Black children potentially internalized negative self-image beliefs while moving to a new neighborhood where the inhabitants appear to "get the hell out" because of their arrival. The schools and public services all went through an unneeded and destructive metamorphosis as the community changed from White to Black.

As Whites fled the inner cities as a result of a few new Black neighbors joining the community, urban neighborhoods began an evolution toward neglect and decay. As urban labor pools became increasingly Black, thousands of inner city, businesses, manufacturers, and service providers moved from these now—predominantly-Black communities, leaving them with few jobs, minimal services, many abandoned and vacant properties, and, in short, economically bankrupt. Before White flight, these communities could substantially support themselves through the production of local goods and services that employed thousands within the community itself, creating very vibrant living environments.

As Blacks moved in and Whites moved out followed by local business entities, the community's economic support base became dependent on Blacks' financial resources generated outside of the community. While many Blacks enjoyed employment in public service, downtown companies and other establishments independent of the community, communities thrive when there is gainful economic stimulus and employment within the community itself. There are always scores of people in any locale who, for whatever reason, need to work locally. When this local job base does not exist, these folks suffer lack of self-worth and become victim to all of the counterproductive activities and behaviors that corrupt an idle person. Once you have a critical mass of people in this predicament, particularly young men, the neighborhood starts to become at risk. Alcohol and drug abuse sets in, gangs form to exploit the drug economy, mindless petty crime and violence erupt from the reduced judgment resulting from intoxicated brains, and the downward spiral continues.

Black neighborhoods gradually became centers of poverty and despair, with drug and gang activity becoming a primary source of economic and social survival for many of the youth of the community. As a result, many Blacks fortunate enough to acquire education and skills valuable to the mainstream have to make a difficult choice, either remain in the community as a role model and potentially risk the safety of your family and property, or move to a more affluent area to provide a better environment for your family and fewer risks to your children.

Welfare

The Crippling Crutch

Welfare, also known as public aid, or Aid to Families with Dependent Children (AFDC) is intended to help people who are temporarily or permanently unable to earn a living and support themselves. For able-bodied people, welfare provides assistance during periods of financial difficulties due to the economy or changing workplace dynamics. Welfare provides a "safety net" that helps people sustain themselves while they seek new employment or develop more marketable skills. Welfare recipients are normally those needing help to support dependent children. In cases of disabled individuals, welfare is intended to provide longer term support. These welfare recipients include elderly people and people with mental or physical disabilities. Generally, in the United States, welfare represents government-funded programs that provide economic support, goods, and services targeted at unemployed or underemployed people.

Welfare as a practical matter works because it targets support at those who are most in economic need. However, welfare creates problematic incentives. For example, if welfare recipients begin to earn more money than they had been earning, but still not enough to sustain themselves, their benefits may fall and their taxes rise. This can be a powerful incentive for recipients to remain on welfare and not seek work, for if your basic need for food, shelter, and health care are covered, why bother with a minimum-wage job and no health care coverage? In effect, this situation creates a penalty for welfare recipients who go to work, especially in any of the many low-wage jobs typically available to them. Working for minimal wage, minus taxes, often cannot offset the loss of welfare benefits and can leave the welfare recipient worse off.

Targeting welfare benefits to certain groups also creates incentives for people to change their behavior in order to become eligible for benefits. A young mother may be less inclined to marry or stay married if single parenthood makes it easier or more beneficial to claim welfare.

Society has traditionally perceived that welfare is a free ride that attracts people looking for an easy life. However, that is clearly not the case, and welfare is not a desirable way of life. Some very dysfunctional people may have used welfare as a "meal ticket," but those people who became habitually dependent on public aid were not a large proportion of its recipients.

There were inherent problems with the welfare system. It did not provide effective means for its recipients to transition back into the workforce and often created disincentives for working. Some recipients felt stigmatized and began to withdraw and isolate themselves from society, furthering their inability to secure employment. Some people became comfortable and settled for the minimal economic existence that welfare enabled. But most able recipients moved beyond welfare since they could not survive on it without supplementary sources of income.

In 1996, Congress enacted various limitations to correct some of the broken entitlements of welfare. The 1996 law replaced Aid to Families with Dependent Children (AFDC) with Temporary Assistance to Needy Families (TANF). The TANF program improved the moral foundation on which welfare was based. It required able-bodied recipients to work or prepare for work in order to retain aid. Though far from perfect, the new welfare law was a substantial improvement.

States were required to place 45 percent of their TANF recipients into work activities or to reduce future caseloads by an equivalent amount. For the first time, state welfare agencies were pushed to engage recipients in work, to reduce public aid dependence, and subsequently their caseloads.

Under TANF reform, Welfare cases dropped significantly, and by the late 1990s, most states had met their federal goals. As a result, states were no longer required to reduce welfare dependency or enforce rigorous work placement requirements. This allowed some states to revert back to simply mailing welfare checks and the progressive effort to reduce dependence and increase employment began to slow. The national TANF caseload has remained fairly constant ever since but still an improvement over the previous welfare system.

For the first time, the 1996 law promoted healthy marriage among public aid recipients. Before the new law, single parenthood had been the principal cause of child poverty and welfare dependence. The welfare system had, for decades, undermined marriage in low-income communities, created disincentives for marriage, and treated fathers as irrelevant. By 1996, over one-third of children were born out of wedlock; among Blacks, the number was 67 percent. Children born out of wedlock are seven times more likely to live in poverty. In addition, growing up without a father in the home has many harmful long-term effects on the development of children. Children raised without fathers are more likely to become involved in crime, to abuse drugs, to become sexually active earlier, to have emotional and behavioral problems, to fail in school, and to end up on welfare themselves.

Some portion of the welfare population is really not employable. These are mildly to moderately disabled people with some having substance abuse problems, mental illness, or moderate retardation. They can't compete for or hold jobs in the private sector or in the public sector. Without public assistance, these people would become the full responsibility of their families or live on the streets.

While more White Americans benefit from the welfare system than African Americans, and much of the country's welfare resources went to support the old and the disabled, African Americans were substantially "crippled" by the welfare system more so than any other group of Americans with the possible exception of the American Indian. While welfare itself is not a problem, when administered to a distinct group of people who are socially stigmatized, culturally detached, and economically shut out, certain trends begin to emerge. Then, when combined with the historically discriminatory and oppressive practices of American society, government, media, and business, it's easy to see how, for some, public aid could become an addictive lifeline that reduces initiative and disrupts the normal human orientation around self-reliance, family, and respect. For some, welfare became an easier path to survival compared to minimum-wage jobs.

The welfare queen is a stereotypical image that many White Americans have in their heads about Black women. It erroneously perceives Black women as living comfortably on welfare while raising a big family without a husband and with children from different fathers. It views Black women as avoiding work, overly promiscuous, and unwilling to better themselves. The irony is that most welfare queens, women living on welfare as a way of life, were not Black but White. Stereotypes are not based on facts, but on messages intended for the stereotype perpetrator to convey.

The Black welfare queen stereotype:

- Supports White perceptions of Blacks as poor, oversexed, and unintelligent
- Deflects the root causes of Black poverty away from whites, allowing the country at large to disassociate itself from Black betterment
- Portrays Black women as having an easy life and getting paid for sitting around having babies
- Reinforces right wing conservatives justification for cutting public spending on the poor and reducing taxes

Until the 1960s, the poor were regularly and accurately presented in mass media as being primarily White. It was in the 1970s that "Black" and "poor" became synonymous, as if there were no poor Whites or affluent Blacks. The term *welfare queen* originated from Ronald Reagan's propaganda when he ran for president in 1976. He told the story of a Cadillac-driving Black woman who used fictitious names, addresses, and social security numbers to steal $150,000 from the welfare system. The press tried to locate this illusive woman, but as it turned out, Reagan's people contrived the story. Unfortunately, the idea of a welfare queen stuck as a convenient stereotype for the White majority to believe. While perceptions regarding welfare and Black women have always been highly exaggerated, the absence of Black fathers is a terrible reality.

Because of the focus of mass media and its ability to perpetuate stereotypes, Blacks became stigmatized with all of the negative connotations that welfare represented. While it is true that a disproportionate number of Blacks as a group received welfare benefits, as a percentage of the total number of welfare recipients, Whites by far represented the largest percentage of folks benefiting from the programs. White is not the typical image of a welfare recipient that the American media created for our society to perceive. The pervasive negative imagery of welfare and African Americans easily allowed the political manipulation of the White majority, to buy into social and political agendas that were anti-welfare, while promoting continued negative stereotypes toward Blacks.

Even today, it is likely that the minds of America's White majority, who embody the economic and institutional power and influence of the country, are still polluted by past media-dominated negative imagery of African Americans. While this imagery is improving in many areas of media today, it will take a few generations of "mental cleansing" for the lingering effect of decades of stereotypical Black images to become less automatic for the majority of the American population, and then only if a reversal of this imagery offsets the reality that has resulted from the negative images, perceptions, and messages of the past. American mass media presented negative imagery and messages for so long against Black America that society as a whole bought into these ideas and perceptions, and even worse, Black America adopted them into their way of life. Undoing the damage to the way society of all ethnicities perceives Black people will be a long-term challenge.

The following are actual pre-1996 Welfare Reform AFDC statistics from the U.S. Census Bureau, last revised, September, 13, 2000:

U.S. Census Bureau—STATISTICAL BRIEF

MOTHERS WHO RECEIVE AFDC PAYMENTS
Fertility and Socioeconomic Characteristics
March 1995 Economics and Statistics Administration, U.S. Department of Commerce

In 1993, the Nation had 36 million mothers 15 to 44 years old; 3.8 million of them were receiving AFDC (Aid to Families with

Dependent Children) payments to help with the rearing of 9.7 million children. (An additional 0.5 million women over 45 years old and 0.3 million fathers living with their dependent children also received AFDC.)

- *Race:* About 1 in 4 Black mothers of childbearing ages (1.5 million) were AFDC recipients, higher than the 7 percent of corresponding White mothers (2.1 million). Despite these differences in recipiency rates, Black AFDC mothers did not have significantly more children than their White counterparts.
- *Hispanic origin:* Nearly 1 in 5 Hispanic mothers (784,000) aged 15 to 44 were on AFDC. By comparison, about 1 in 10 (3.0 million) non-Hispanic mothers were AFDC recipients. Although both Hispanic and non-Hispanic mothers on AFDC were an average of 20 years old when they had their first child, Hispanic women had almost 0.7 more children than non-Hispanic women. About 3 in 10 Hispanic mothers on AFDC were born outside the United States.
- *Nativity:* About 9 percent (392,000) of the Nation's 4.2 million foreign-born mothers aged 15-44 were on AFDC, not statistically different from the 11 percent (3.4 million) of U.S.-born mothers who were AFDC recipients. Native—and foreign born mothers on AFDC each had higher fertility rates than their counterparts who were not AFDC participants. Incidentally, about three-quarters of all foreign-born mothers on AFDC were not citizens of the United States.

Most AFDC mothers are jobless . . .

- Unlike mothers not getting AFDC payments, most AFDC mothers (87 percent) didn't have a job. On average, jobless AFDC mothers supported 2.6 children each, no more than AFDC mothers who had a job for all or part of the month preceding the survey.
- Nearly three-quarters of mothers on AFDC lived in families with monthly incomes of less than $1,000; these low-income mothers supported an average of 2.7 children

each. In contrast, only 10 percent of non-AFDC mothers lived in families with such low incomes; these low-income non-AFDC mothers had an average of 2.2 children each. About 4 in every 5 AFDC mothers were below the poverty level.

Affirmative Action

The Big Tease

You do not take a person who, for years, has been hobbled by chains and liberate him, bring him up to the starting line of a race and say, "you are free to compete with all the others," and still justly believe that you have been completely fair.
–President Lyndon B. Johnson, Howard University, 1965

Affirmative action could have been the policy that "leveled the playing field" if it had been applied widely enough and aggressively enough. Several policies were created in the United States that were intended to increase opportunities for minorities and women by granting them increased participation in institutional and corporate employment and promotion, college and university admissions, and the awarding of government and public sector contracts.

Generally, affirmative action is an attempt by government, business, and institutions to remedy the effects of past discrimination against an underrepresented group of society. In practice, many elements of society do not embrace the need to "do the right thing" for those historically oppressed and views many applications of affirmative action as simply reverse discrimination against the White majority, and White men in particular. This perspective is symptomatic of the power possessed by the White majority to promote what is self-serving:

- When slavery was in the interest of the nation, it was a good thing
- As slavery began to divide the nation, it became a bad thing
- When the civil rights movement began to disrupt the fabric of society, affirmative action became a good thing
- In times of civil rest, affirmative action is viewed to take opportunities away from White majority members allegedly more deserving
- Blacks are more readily received into collegiate and professional sports and entertainment, where their performance directly links to increased revenue

And that is the way it has gone for Blacks in America. The policies, programs, and legislation that promotes the interest of members of the White majority is the position that the self-serving majority members take. This is not to say that all White Americans subscribe to this self-serving mind-set, for many of the White majority are themselves responsible for conceptualizing and promoting equitable ideas and views that materialize into fair practices in our institutions. Unfortunately though, powerful influences emerge from the majority's far right that stifles the progress that the nation has made in developing a mainstream-oriented Black population.

The point of this writing is that if the time, resources, and effort are not expended for the cause of reconstructing Black America now, we may never again live in a time where the root causes of Black life ailments are alive and understood. As a result, the desire for corrective action would be lost forever since the basis for it would have long since been forgotten, moved out of the public psyche, and dissolved. Once that occurs, not only will there be no support for Black life equality, but many will associate the condition of most Blacks with a lack of inherent abilities rather than the evolution of a subculture resulting from hundreds of years of discriminatory practices and an oppressive environment.

Before the 1960s, Blacks were prevented from entering many corporate and institutional jobs and educational opportunities. The Civil Rights Act of 1964 was the first legislation aimed at correcting this inequality. Title VII of the Civil Rights Act specifically prohibited discrimination in employment and created an environment in which affirmative action could be born. The Equal Employment Opportunity Commission (EEOC), created by the Civil Rights Act of 1964, and the Office of Federal Contract Compliance became an important enforcement agency for affirmative action. The significance of this event while self-serving the White majority at the time is that progress was made for thousands of African Americans even if a significant degree of regression came later. Every attempt that society makes to support Black America does render some African Americans better off as a result. However, the impact of discriminatory practices in America against Blacks runs broad and deep. It will require a focused concentrated effort and resources to be consistently applied over a long period of time to rectify the oppressive past in a meaningful way.

The periodic rise of anti-affirmative action sentiment causes society to take a step backward and is an impediment to the continuity of Black's pursuit of substantial participation in mainstream America. This is evidenced in both federal and state politics. For example:

- In 1995, the regents of the University of California voted to end all affirmative action in hiring and admissions for the entire state university system. As a result, African American enrollment in the system's entering undergraduate class plummeted in 1998 when the changes took effect
- In 1996, California voters approved Proposition 209, an initiative that ended affirmative action throughout the state in public hiring, purchasing, and other government business, which caused a 63 percent drop in the number of African American enrolled in UC Law Schools and a 26 percent drop in UC Business School African American enrollments
- In 1996, the Fifth U.S. Circuit Court barred the University of Texas Law School from "any consideration of race or ethnicity" in its admissions decisions. As in California, the termination of affirmative action at the University of Texas Law School led to a drop in African American enrollment by more than 20 percent
- In 1998, Washington state voters passed Initiative 200 to ban affirmative action in state and local government hiring, contracting, and education

You can see from these scenarios that legislatures, the courts, and the public have been divided over affirmative action, and the status of affirmative action remains uncertain and shifts by the influence of the current power structures.

The term *affirmative action* was first used by President John F. Kennedy in a 1961 executive order designed to encourage contractors on projects financed with federal funds to racially integrate their workforces. Kennedy's executive order declared that federal contractors should "take affirmative action to ensure that applicants are employed, and employees are treated during their employment, without regard to race, creed, color or national origin." The original objective of the civil rights movement was "color-blind" laws. However, simply ending a long-standing policy of discrimination did not go far enough. Affirmative or proactive measures to increase equality were more necessary.

From its beginning in the United States, affirmative action has been highly controversial. Critics charge that affirmative action policies, which give preferential treatment to people based on their membership in a group, violate the principle that all individuals are equal under the law. These critics argue that it is unfair to discriminate against members of one group today to compensate for discrimination against other groups in the past. They regard affirmative action as reverse discrimination that unfairly prevents Whites and men from being hired and promoted. This again is the self-serving consciousness of the majority White America, for if this "fair mindedness" had previously been the dominant thinking, then hundreds of years would not have passed before any level of equality had been accomplished for Blacks. Where was this thinking then?

Advocates of affirmative action would argue that discrimination is, by definition, unfair treatment of people because they belong to a certain group. Therefore, effective remedies must systematically aid groups that have suffered from discrimination. Supporters contend that affirmative action policies are the only way to ensure an integrated society in which all segments of the population have an equal opportunity to share in jobs, education, and other benefits. They argue that numerical goals for hiring, promotions, and college admissions are necessary to integrate fields traditionally closed to women and minorities because of discrimination. Anything short of quantitative measurement would have no basis of management and control since all intangible valuations of progress would be highly subjective.

It seems reasonable that if some African Americans are allowed to obtain a position at the expense of a majority member, the net effect to society would be more positive since those African American individuals and their future generations would have a significantly greater chance to participate in mainstream America, which is entirely dominated by the White majority today. So while technically a specific occurrence of "reverse discrimination" may be unfair to the White majority member in a specific event, the "greater good" for society dictates that the collective positive net effect should be pursued if we are ever to enter the realm of social equity.

The question becomes, how long do you promote affirmative action with its preferential treatment of minorities and women before the privilege scale begins to tip the other way? Based on statistics reflecting governmental, institutional, and corporate financial power and control favoring Whites, and considering over three hundred years of overt oppression and one hundred years discrimination rendering Blacks nearly permanently in an underclass status, it is reasonable, albeit not practical, to estimate that one hundred years of varying degrees of affirmative action practices (separate from reconstruction) could be considered and would not detrimentally impact the established power base of American industry, government, and institutions currently and permanently disproportionately controlled by White America. However, this dynamic is changing today due to the meteoric increase in the Hispanic population and the eventual impact they will have on all of America. That though is the subject for another book.

Considering the self-serving consciousness of majority White America and their inability to embrace affirmative action concepts to a revolutionary degree, a very compelling case needs to be developed that clearly withstands any "reasonable man" argument, whose benefits could be holistically promoted for the value that it represents to the betterment of society as a whole.

The scope and limitations of affirmative action policy were defined through legislative decisions by the Supreme Court of the United States. While some organizations adopted fair hiring policies and practices in the "spirit" of doing the right thing, for many others the adoption of hiring policies and practices to increase African American participation was mainly to avoid penalties and discrimination lawsuits, which, again, is evidence of the self-serving consciousness of majority White America and an indication that unless forced to change, people will do what they are more comfortable doing.

While the Supreme Court consistently upheld the constitutionality of affirmative action, it did place some restrictions on its implementation. The following are a few cases in point:

The Supreme Court's ruling in Regents of the University of California v. Bakke (1978) declared that it was unconstitutional for the medical school of the University of California at Davis to establish a rigid quota system by reserving a certain number of places in each class for minorities. However, the ruling upheld the right of schools to consider a variety of factors when evaluating applicants, including race, ethnicity, gender, and economic status.

In United Steelworkers v. Weber (1979) the court ruled that a short-term voluntary training program that gave preference to minorities was constitutional. The court reasoned that a temporary program designed to remedy specific past discriminatory practices did not unduly restrict the advancement of Whites.

In Fullilove v. Klutznick (1980) the Supreme Court upheld a provision of the Public Works Employment Act of 1977, which provided a 10 percent "set-aside" for hiring African American contractors on federally funded public works projects. The majority of the justices believed that the Congress of the United States has special powers to remedy past and ongoing discrimination in the awarding of federal contracts.

Conservative justices appointed to the Supreme Court by Republican presidents in the 1980s and 1990s have attempted to limit the scope of affirmative action. Although very divided on the issue, the court has struck down a number of affirmative action programs as unfair or too broad in their application. The following are examples of these cases:

In Wygant v. Jackson Board of Education (1986) the Supreme Court struck down a plan to protect minority teachers from layoffs at the expense of White teachers with greater seniority.

In Richmond v. J. A. Croson Co. (1989) the court rejected a local set-aside program for minority contractors, ruling that local governments do not have the same power as Congress to enact such programs.

In Ward's Cove Packing Company v. Antonio (1989), the Supreme Court revised the standards established by the 1971 Griggs decision. The Ward's Cove decision required that employees filing discrimination lawsuits demonstrate that specific hiring practices had led to racial disparities in the workplace. Even if this could be shown, these hiring practices would still be legal if they served "legitimate employment goals of the employer."

In the 1990s, affirmative action had been a highly charged legal and political issue causing Congress to respond to a number of conservative rulings by the Supreme Court by passing the Civil Rights Act of 1991, which strengthened antidiscrimination laws and largely reversed the Wards Cove decision.

In Metro Broadcasting v. Federal Communications Commission (1990) the court upheld federal laws designed to increase the number of minority-owned radio and television stations.

In Adarand Constructors v. Peña (1995) the Supreme Court examined a federal statute that reserved "not less than 10 percent" of funds provided for highway construction for small businesses owned by "socially and economically disadvantaged individuals." The court's majority opinion, written by Sandra Day O'Connor, overturned the statute and declared that even federal affirmative action programs are constitutional only when they are "narrowly tailored" to serve a "compelling government interest."

It is clear to see from these cases that affirmative action has been a complex and controversial topic for many years. The United

States president, Congress, and Supreme Court have gone back and forth on this matter largely depending on the conservative or liberal mind-set of the governing bodies at the time.

Largely, the U.S. government has demonstrated the right intent at the high level. However, on the ground where real people collide, even the strongest affirmative action laws, policies, and practices are no match for any ill-intended goal of people who are in a position of influence and who are antiaffirmative action.

At the ground level, there are so many subtle ways to disrupt the livelihood, peace, and happiness of someone in the workforce completely "under the radar" of affirmative action. And when you consider the preconceived notions and stereotypes that people hold against each other, you realize that the fairness intended from affirmative action can't be a self-policing concept. For it's one thing to have laws on the books, it's quite another to promote the spirit of the law in everyday interaction between people.

If the attitude of individuals in powerful and influential positions is not good, fair, and constructive, there is no way to measure how undermining they can be to the common good of society. In other words, you cannot legislate against racism, bigotry, and prejudice, for these are in the hearts of people and affect their everyday interactions. This is one reason why strong, pervasive, and measureable affirmative action is crucial. There are people in society who systematically negate the impact of affirmative action. While many do benefit from affirmative action, many more are victims of the backlash resulting from affirmative action when it is administered by those who oppose it and may resent those who benefit from it.

Affirmative action was effective at producing two results. First, the critical mass of the Black middle class can be almost entirely associated with the progress of affirmative action, with the exception of labor opportunities generated by the steel and assembly plants in the north during our automotive glory days. Since before Affirmation Action was introduced and enforced, most employers had no incentive to hire and promote Blacks, and their hiring managers generally held prejudiced attitudes that were commonplace in our nation. However, an occasional hiring manager was either a fair and reasonable person whose independent mind had not been polluted and negatively influenced by the abundance of negativity associated with Black people. These influential people chose to judge the employment candidates by the content of their character rather than the color of their skin.

There have always been companies of good integrity or that possessed a strong interest in the communities that they serve or sell products into. Examples of these include Allstate Insurance, IBM, and McDonald's. These companies and others like them took it upon themselves to provide ample opportunities to minorities and women. The other more prevalent case where African Americans were aptly employed is where there was a need for labor usually in the form of manual, maintenance, or administrative duties that were typically dead-end jobs where Blacks would toil for their entire working life with no chance for upward mobility.

The second result of affirmative action is the negative resentful sentiment created and festered in some White Americans who had become aggravated by the perception that all of these "unqualified" Blacks were taking their jobs and promotions. They possess a general opinion that this person or that person is only in the position that they are in because they are Black. This belief harbored great resentment in many Whites in the workplace, causing some of them to make work life for an unlucky Black person difficult at best. When you combine the sense of privilege and entitlement that Whites typically enjoy by simply being in the majority, and the favor that then comes along with being a part of a group that has power and influence, it becomes easy for a person with that reality to act out on resentful feelings and negative beliefs that they have about someone who is virtually powerless in the same environment.

While Blacks have achieved to some degree valuable access to good jobs as a result of affirmative action, many Blacks are exposed to abusive environments that many times leave them feeling vulnerable and powerless. Because of the harsh feelings of many Whites who are in the workplace and the negative stereotypical beliefs that they hold consciously or subconsciously, it is difficult for many Blacks to really excel in corporate America and take full advantage of their newly found opportunities. While affirmative action got many people in the door, it cannot achieve the most important opportunity creating feat, which is to create strong lasting relationships for Blacks with Whites in positions of power and influence. While companies and institutions may have had to hire minorities and support diversity initiatives, the managers and executives do not have to befriend them and invite them over for dinner or to the club. And therein lays the "glass ceiling." In our society, real opportunities emerge as a result of close relationships with influential people who mentor, endorse, and sponsor your progress. Most African Americans do not have those types of relationships.

It may be true that during the affirmative action era, some African Americans may have obtained employment and promotion opportunities when they were not fully qualified. However, this happens within White America all of the time. Most people know of companies, state and local governments, small businesses, etc., where family members, friends, and associates of someone of influence got a job there because of who they know. Whenever someone believes a person is in that position only because they are Black, they need to realize that most Whites are in their positions only because they are White. If they were Black, regardless of their qualifications, they probably would not be where they are today. Being Black historically excluded you from the candidate pool of real opportunities, while being White historically allowed your inclusion.

The following are a few facts regarding affirmative action and its relevance and benefits to society:

- White men are only 43% of the Fortune 2000 workforce, but they hold 95% of high level and executive management jobs. And this is with Affirmative Action in place

- White men make up 48% of the college-educated workforce, but hold more than 80% of the top jobs in U.S. corporations, law firms, college faculty, government, and news media
- Affirmative Action attempts to level the playing field so African Americans, and others, have the chance to compete in education and in business
- Of 3000 federal court decisions in discrimination cases between 1990 and 1994, only 100 (.2%) were claims of reverse discrimination, and only 6 of those were found to be valid. Affirmative Action is not significantly impacting the White majority
- Despite the enormous gains made by the civil rights movements, African Americans still face unfair obstacles in education and business opportunities
- Affirmative Action is an investment in the future. The white majority is declining in numbers. By the time the college graduating class of 2010 are at the midpoint of their careers, the U.S. population will be comprised of more than one third African Americans and Hispanics
- Affirmative Action helps open doors for African Americans who often don't have connections the way the children of college alumni get preferential treatment, or friends who help friends and acquaintances get jobs through influential social networks
- Affirmative Action programs acknowledge that hundreds of years of discrimination cannot be erased in a few decades without support. Affirmative Action is the bridge between changing the laws and changing the culture
- Eliminating affirmative action leads to the re-segregation of higher education. When affirmative action was outlawed at the University of Texas in 1995, the number of black students at the UT Law School dropped from 65 in 1996 to 11 in 1997 and Latino student enrollments have been cut in half since the decision
- Between 1981 and 2001, the total number of college degrees awarded to Native Americans rose by 151.9% because of affirmative action policies

Sources:
   CivilRights.org
   U.S. Department of Education
   U.S. Census Bureau

Assimilation

Michael Jackson, Black or White?

RKS 2010

While Michael Jackson was obviously an African American, to look at him in the years leading to his death, without knowledge of his origin, you would not know what ethnicity he was or how to classify him. All physical characteristics of his person had been altered over the years and, in some cases, extremely. His skin became whiter than white, his nose became narrower, his hair became straight, and his lips became thin.

Michael Jackson appears to have attempted to transform himself into a White person. Why would he do that? What did Michael Jackson experience in the formative years of his life that had such a profound psychological impact on him, that he would decide he no longer wanted to be what God made him, but rather take on a completely different physical appearance?

In the introduction chapter "A Mind is a Horrible Thing to Waste," I describe my own coming to terms with my Blackness as a five-year-old boy growing up during the civil rights movement and being exposed, at a vulnerable age, to the obvious and dramatic rejection that awaited me based on the color of my skin.

Michael Jackson and I were born in the same year. He as well would have been exposed to similar negative visual stimuli during the chaotic times of the civil rights movement during the 1960s. In fact, as Michael became a traveling member of the Jackson 5 band, he may have had a compounding of related exposure as he and his brothers traveled around the country from state to state, hotel to hotel, and venue to venue.

As recently as the 1970s, and even later in the South, there are many accounts of Black entertainers who were subjected to ridicule and second-class citizenship as they traveled, and attempted to arrange appropriate accommodations for food and lodging. Who knows what kind of racial messages Michael was exposed to and internalizing when he was an eight-, nine-, or ten-year-old boy with direct exposure to all aspects of U.S. society during the late 1960s and early 1970s. This all happened as he entered the vulnerable years of his adolescence and identity formation.

What messages did Michael perceive in the world of entertainment where, traditionally, the members of acts that "crossed over" into national popularity had certain "White oriented" physical characteristics, which were more acceptable in mainstream society? While Michael broke barriers that other artists had not been able to before him, he did not become universally successful until his skin became lighter and lighter. This need to assimilate mainstream America had preceded Michael Jackson with various other artists in the Motown lineup. However, none had completely modified their physical traits the way Michael had.

Michael Jackson's perceived need to transform into a White person was probably not a normal choice of personal expression, but more likely the result of a centuries-old societal race-relations dynamic that imprints self-hatred in the minds of African Americans through exposure to governmental acts, mass media presentations, and public institutions, which would promote and support the alienation and control of Black U.S. citizens.

The profound self-contemptuous attitudes among many African Americans are not without rational explanation. It is the result of years of oppression and discrimination. The culprit has been the mainstream media's implementation of a manipulative system that has been used for maintaining the White statuesque. It has been a tool diligently implemented by the America's ruling elite who actually run our country.

These aristocratic groups of wealthy White Americans demonstrate sustained power and influence as a means to their personal ends, regardless of who is actually president. Their influence impacts our daily life in ways we don't even understand, from the media messages we get, to the political positions we take, to the wars we fight, and possibly worse.

Much of this groups influence has been historically perpetuated through the nation's mass media outlets. It distorts the portrayal of African Americans and amplifies negative perceptions to the point of becoming a mass media psychosocial manipulation program that ensures that Blacks remain predominantly racially devalued, unaccepted, and, most importantly, economically exploited.

America's extreme forms of exploitation and Black's perceived need to assimilate is born from the fact that mass media forms, for all of us, our perceptions and image of the world and everything we think we know.

Most information outside of our personal lives comes to us via newspapers, magazines, radio, or television, and now, the internet. Through these avenues, the mass media has unlimited influence for guiding our thoughts and opinions. Their influence is implemented by the way the news is covered, which points of view are emphasized or deemphasized, the phrasing of headlines, and the choice of words, pictures, and illustrations. All of these practices subliminally and profoundly affect the way we interpret what we see or hear.

Black images of themselves have been greatly influenced by what the media has shown about their own group and has manipulated the minds of the Black masses to admire Whites while rejecting themselves, hence Black on Black crime. An example to make this point is that in most African nations, White life is more valuable than Black life even to Black people. So if you visit Africa as a Black person, you are more at risk than if you visit as a White person. This little known fact is also true in most urban ghettos of the United States.

The historical bombardment of deplorable negative images of themselves that African Americans are constantly inundated with has been a deliberate psychological conditioning program designed to destroy African Americans' sense of Black racial heritage, pride, and unity by subjecting them to only the worst in themselves while presenting White images in a way that instills confidence, admiration, and respect.

This daily assault on the Black psyche disrupted the African Americans' sense of self-esteem and racial unity. It ingrained self-hatred, self-doubt, and distrust among themselves. The psychosocial impact from the mass media portrayals of Blacks has, over time, manipulated Black people into a reality where it is now they themselves who are their worst enemy. Black's negative and self-destructive interactions with each other and in their communities serve as evidence to confirm the nearly irreparable damage done to the race.

The need for African Americans to assimilate was absolutely necessary since even when successful, a Black person could only expect to earn a basic living and would still be at the back of the pack where opportunities and upward mobility were concerned. The inability to assimilate normally meant a meager existence scraping a living in the labor-intensive bowels of society, which is where the majority of African Americans existed for hundreds of years.

The Black struggle to assimilate is evident as you look back through historical journals and films and see by the way Blacks dressed, wore their hair, spoke and behaved, that they were trying as best they could to "fit" into the White-controlled society, for it is within the White-controlled society that a decent living could be achieved.

Examples of assimilation can be seen throughout Black history, including the way artist and entertainers presented themselves, the classroom photographs of schoolchildren, pictures in family photo albums, and the scores of news reports and journals showing Black citizens down through the years. Except for the color of their skin, Black Americans conformed to the timely social norms of White America in terms of personal presentation, occupational pursuits, fashion and apparel, and acceptable social behavior. Even during civil rights movement marches, you would see very well-mannered, conservatively dressed, articulate Blacks struggling for equality.

Unfortunately, the assimilation attempts of Blacks for five or six generations since slavery were regularly ignored, unaccepted, and unappreciated by mainstream America. During this period where Blacks really badly wanted to fit in and be a part of their homeland, their homeland was persistently marginalizing them and not embracing them into the productive, constructive process of the American socioeconomic climb.

Stereotype Threat

Subconscious Intimidation

When capable Black college students fail to perform as well as their White counterparts, the explanation often has less to do with preparation or ability than with the threat of stereotypes about their capacity to succeed.

—Claude M. Steele, Psychologist

Stereotype threat is the fear that an individual's behavior will conform to a *stereotype* associated with the group with which the individual identifies. This fear can sometimes affect an individual's performance. It causes an individual to feel at risk of confirming, as self-characteristic, a negative stereotype about one's group as perceived by others. Stereotype threat shackles the minds of millions of otherwise productive, high-performing Blacks every day, causing them to become less vocal and relevant, productive, successful, and fulfilled.

The stereotype threat concept was first theorized by psychologist Claude Steele.[20] Stereotype threat concludes that when a fixed physical characteristic like race or gender is acknowledged in a given situation that requires individual performance, like taking a test, public speaking, etc., the individual's subsequent performance is often adversely affected as a result of the stereotype-aware psychological tension generated at the time of the event. Hence, according to Steele, "culturally shared stereotypes suggesting poor performance of certain groups can, when made salient in a context involving the stereotype, disrupt performance of an individual who identifies with that group" (Steele, Aronson 1995).

Although Steele and Aronson focused their emphasis on race affecting test performance, similar studies proved equal results when the emphasis is on gender. In some studies, researchers found that "consistent exposure to stereotype threat (e.g., faced by some ethnic minorities in academic environments and women in math) can reduce the degree to which individuals value the domain in question" (Aronson 2002; Steele 1997). Also, similar research found that there are varying degrees by which an individual of a certain group is affected by stereotype threat. Some members may be more vulnerable to its negative consequences than others based on the strength of one's group identification. This variable depends on how "shielded" the member was from negative influences during their developmental years. Research has proven that when an individual identifies with a specific group, performance can

---

[20] Claude Mason Steele is a social psychology professor at Stanford University, where he has taught since 1991. He is best known for his work on stereotype threat.

be negatively affected because of concerns that they will, in fact, confirm the negative stereotypes of that group.

Claude Steele and Joshua Aronson articulated the mechanism of "stereotype threat" that contributes to test performance of minority groups. In one study, Steele and Aronson (1995) administered the Graduate Record Examination to European American and African American students. Half of each group was told that their intelligence was being measured while the other half did not know what the test was measuring. The European American students performed almost equally in the two conditions of the experiment. African Americans, in contrast, performed far worse than they otherwise would have when they were told their intelligence was being measured. The researchers concluded that this was because stereotype threat made the students anxious about confirming the stereotype regarding African American IQ. The researchers found that the difference was even more noticeable when race was emphasized.

Steele and Aronson found that high-ability African American student's performance was negatively affected while being tested on cognitive ability, when race is made prominent. Steele wrote that the "stigma" of being African American is substantial and has an effect on the educational performance of African American students. The stereotype that African Americans test poorly can be extremely harmful. Stereotype threats can seriously alter the academic achievement and motivation of an individual.

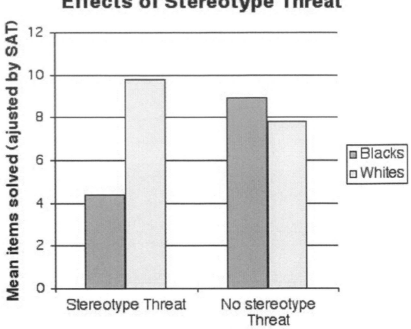

Effects of Stereotype Threat

http://en.wikipedia.org/wiki/File:Stereotype_threat_bw.jpg

In 1995, an experiment leveraging college sophomores at Stanford University was conducted and showed the impact of stereotype threat by asking students to fill out a form indicating their race before taking the test. The following is a synopsis:

> The variable manipulated was whether or not participants were required to list their race before taking the test. In an earlier test, 75% of the Black participants in the diagnostic condition refused to record their race on the questionnaire when given the option, whereas all of the participants in the other conditions did. On the assumption that this was a sign of their stereotype avoidance, it was reasoned that having participants record their race just prior to the test should prime the racial stereotype about ability for Black participants, and thus make them stereotype threatened. If this threat alone is sufficient to impair their performance, then, with SATs covaried, these

participants should perform worse than White participants in this condition.

In the non-stereotype-threat conditions, the demographic questionnaire simply omitted the item requesting participants' race and, otherwise, followed the nondiagnostic procedures. Without raising the specters of ability or race-relevant evaluation, Black participants in this condition were expected to experience no stereotype threat and to perform (adjusted for SATs) on par with White participants.

Thus the predicament of 'stereotype vulnerability': The group members then know that anything about them or anything they do that fits the stereotype can be taken as confirming it as self-characteristic, in the eyes of others, and perhaps even in their own eyes. This vulnerability amounts to jeopardy of double devaluation: once for whatever bad thing the stereotype-fitting behavior or feature would say about anyone, and again for its confirmation of the bad things alleged in the stereotype.

—Claude M. Steele

The mental conditioning resulting from the African American experience down through the years has left a lingering impact on the African American psyche. Many African Americans have "chains on their minds." Stereotype threat is closely related to and compounded with the mental condition called "Twosome" termed by W. E. B. Dubois[21] and described earlier in the introduction to this book. With Twosome, many African Americans are always consciously aware of their Blackness in addition to their regular consciousness as they operate as a person. Layered onto this dysfunctional mental condition is the additional mental baggage of stereotype threat when the African American finds himself

---

[21] William Edward Burghardt DuBois, born February 23, 1868, was an African American educator and leader of the movement for black equality. He was the first African American to earn a Ph.D. from Harvard University in 1895.

or herself in a situation where their performance is likely to be scrutinized.

These are just two acknowledged inhibitors to the peak performance of African Americans, which has been imposed on them through years of discrimination and oppression. We will never know how constructive and productive African American's could have become if they had not been burdened with this legacy of self-limiting psychological shackles. It's one thing to have your abilities and potential shattered due to factors outside of your control (i.e., slavery, racism, discrimination, etc.). It is quite a different matter to have your abilities and potential limited due to the self-imposed restrictions that occur in your own mind. This reality is very unfortunate considering present time, for as the forces external to the individual, which previously inhibited African American success are being lifted, and relief has finally come by way of a more diversified, inclusive, and tolerant society, many African Americans carry around excess mental baggage which causes automatic self-induced performance limitations that affects their communications and/or behavior and the associated results and perceptions that are produced.

While many Blacks do freely operate in the mainstream culture relatively uninhibited by mental baggage, it is the exceptional ones, particularly if they are born before 1970, who possess the array of professional and social skills, as well as the variety of well-rounded experiences that enable them to thrive and excel regardless of this added weight that many feel. And even in those cases, you have to wonder how great they may have become if the topics in this book were not an issue at all.

The Rap Era

Self Victimization

Since slavery, many generations of African Americans have played by the rules and strived to assimilate as best they could into the socioeconomic structure of the United States of America. These past generations have for the most part been repeatedly and consistently rejected and/or marginalized by White America, leaving many of their descendants socioeconomically deprived today. And now, Black youth don't seem to care anymore.

As a way of dealing with the hopelessness, despair, and overall oppressive environmental effects in the Black community, rap began as a positive and constructive social movement through musical beats and rhyme and spread like wildfire throughout young Black America. Unfortunately, rap, a subset of hip-hop, over the course of twenty-five years or so, deteriorated into one of the most destructive and venomous ingredients to ever inflict the Black community.

Originally, most rap artists and their content projected positive messages to its following, and very few had negative derogatory vibes. Much of rap's original messages aimed to educate people politically regarding how to raise Black America from its doldrums. The tides turned over time. Recently, much of rap's imagery and content has been extremely derogatory and harmful while a sliver of the rap industry tries to keep it constructive with positive messages.

During the birth of rap in the late seventies and early eighties, many of the original rappers created rhymes with meaningful lyrics that promoted love and respect, education, and self-sufficiency. Through their art, these early rappers criticized the negative characters and influences that plagued the Black community and had a healthy emcee competition developing between them. The early rappers were mostly positive and constructive members of the Black community and included artists such as Kool Moe Dee, the Sugarhill Gang, Grandmaster Flash, Run-D.M.C., Brother D, and Collective Efforts, just to name a few. While some of their art illustrated the sultriness required for partying and dancing, they spent ample time setting a positive tone and vibe for listeners to groove to.

As time went on and hip-hop evolved, something changed. Somehow, while hip-hop remains a vibrant and constructive art form, some rap, became a very derogatory subset. Gangsta rap in particular, began to sensationalize and glorify the negative characteristics represented in ghetto communities. The rap movement significantly shifted from "building a positive self and community" to "this negative shit is our reality so deal with it."

Unfortunately, the negativity projected by some rap artist still possessed the melodic rhythmic beats that made the medium appealing to the masses, but the messages became largely degrading and demoralizing. The result became a cascading of antisocial ideas deep into the psyche of developing youth. These unsuspecting youth, many of whom are already marginalized and posses little hope of a mainstream life, buy into the messages and images created by the new wave rap artist and incorporate the implied persona into their language, dress, choices, and behavior.

Rap's negative turn has had a very unfortunate impact on the Black community in particular although the effects are spilling over into society at large. The way women and girls are referred to and treated, the quick use of violence and guns for any minor altercation or conflict, the improper use of language, the sloppy flamboyant dress code, the antisociety attitudes, the party-all-the-time lifestyle, the general lack of contributions that productively and constructively benefit society, have all become the way of life for an entire generation of Black youth, with some exceptions including those who are either lucky enough to have a family structure that "shields" them to some degree; or fortunate enough to have the personal drive and ambition that focuses and leads them out of the chaos without getting distracted and "snagged" by the negative environment through random violence, blighted community environments, deteriorating schools, inappropriate, ill-intended friendships and associations, drugs and sex, dysfunctional families, or any of the many other, to use a metaphor, "crabs" in the Black ghetto "barrel" that keeps one from getting out.

Conforming to the negative elements of rap may be the most significant deterrent to the productive development of constructive Black youth. Young people are not likely to have a mind-set oriented toward medicine, law, science, physics, astronomy, engineering, etc., if their focus is on violence, sex, drugs, materialism, and otherwise irresponsible behavior.

Rap today can sometimes be a form of Black self-hatred. Black rappers, who portray Black women as "bitches" and "whores" and show respect for Black men only in relation to their capacity for crime and violence are propagating self-hate and racial stereotypes through their music. In addition, some rap has a tendency to propagate negative imagery, which characterizes Black people as physically abusive, users of drugs, lazy, poor parents, bad children, lower intelligence, and with little or no value toward contributing to society in more productive ways.

The evolution and adoption of the rap art form of the hip-hop culture has had mass appeal across the youth of America. While originally adopted by Black youth, rap has become accepted by youth of all ethnicities and has spread to many nations around the world. However, Black youth is more likely to establish a "rap-based" identity since in many cases, it is their primary cultural exposure.

There are pros and cons to the way rap has been embraced. One pro is the obvious wealth that has been created by individuals who statistically may not have otherwise been successful in simply earning a middle-class living, let alone generating wealth. Many rappers have gone on to become very successful businessmen and women who have branched off into a variety of business ventures and enterprises. Many opportunities have opened up to those rappers smart enough to parlay their success into other business areas within and outside of music entertainment. These ventures include but are not limited to television, movies, clothing, fragrances, sports, financial services, beverages, and spirits to name a few. This phenomenon is most respectful and constructive since these entrepreneurs are gaining very valuable domestic and international business experience that can, over time, develop into Black-owned and operated conglomerates on a scale that may reach the level of the S&P 500. This would clearly be forward progress for the few Black enterprises adept enough to continue to achieve excellence.

One con is that many rappers are individuals who are not very intellectual or socially sophisticated and bring "street" attitudes and behavior with them to more affluent venues in society where they are not likely to fit, and unfortunately, they are also not likely to care whether or not they fit, which exacerbates the problem. The perceptions that many of these characters create in the mainstream potentially has a ripple effect back to the Black community in ways the rappers may not be aware of. For example, at the social economic level that some of these rappers operate, they are exposed to many people of other backgrounds who are wealthy, powerful, and influential people in their own right. Many may own companies, or are in positions in organizations where they influence decision making. When it comes to hiring Blacks, at any level of an organization, these individual who have had their impressions consciously or subconsciously impacted by exposure to the street behavior and ignorance of some Black rappers, may generally act according to these perceptions, and unfairly generally apply them to all Blacks. This is human nature. Only the most objective well-meaning human being can cancel out negative stereotypical imagery associated with an individual and not let it affect their judgment. So while many rappers are "living large," they inadvertently are helping keep Blacks as a whole down.

Another con is that unlike the youth of many other ethnicities, African American youth are more likely to become victims of rap's persuasion. The lifestyle depicted in much of rap glamorizes "thug" like behavior, sexual promiscuity, drugs and alcohol, crime and violence. Particularly in the Black ghettos, there are few productive influences to counterbalance the inclination of Black youth to proceed with choices influenced by rap and move in a different direction instead.

Because of all of the ill effects mentioned in this book, and others not represented here, many African American youth in high-risk environments are completely susceptible, without any means of filtering the penetrating illusion of rap's allure.

Boys and girls in the United States of other ethnicities and nationalities generally have more structure in their lives whether it's a prouder heritage, the involvement of two parents, exposure to working adults, many professionals, environments that are relatively clean and safe, decent schools and public facilities, and the list goes on.

While rap appeals to youth in all facets of society, many Whites live in an environment that offers more choices, opportunities, and hope. For the young Black kid, rap becomes a way of life. In many cases, that's all they know and understand, and they generally are not exposed to other ways of life, clean orderly communities, different people, other lifestyles, productive occupations, healthy relationships, loving functional families, self-respect, effective education, healthy lifestyle choices, and orderly conduct.

In short, many Black youth have very little exposure outside of their limited world and experiences, they are ignorant to broader better choices, and they are attracted to and entertained by rap in a way that it becomes who they are and what they do as opposed to simply being a form of entertainment. This of course may affect the rest of their lives since the image projected by someone who has subscribed to the rap lifestyle does not fit into mainstream society. It also becomes very difficult to gain legitimate employment and almost impossible to start a career with upward mobility, since a prerequisite would be the ability to adapt and apply good judgment. So as a consequence, many Black youth end up floundering on the bottom rung of society never really able to achieve upward mobility. And once you introduce babies into the equation, the situation becomes even more dismal and the poverty and despair gets perpetuated into yet another generation.

The end result of rap's negative impact is an environment where dysfunction is perpetuated and becomes normal. That is what is occurring in many Black ghetto communities, which are plagued with:

- single-parent homes with a female struggling to survive economically

- daily doses of gangs, drugs, and senseless violence
- regular shootings and killings over petty issues and conflicts
- teenage pregnancies becoming badges of honor, leaving the young mother possibly poverty stricken for life
- young men frequently valuing thug life and being cool over education which leads to constructive occupations

In addition, Black citizens with more economic resources frequently become victims in their own neighborhood because of the modest signs of middle-class materialism that their lifestyle affords them, causing them to subsequently abandon the Black community before something unfortunate happens.

The negative traits in the Black community, which are reinforced by rap, are on a downward spiral and spinning out of control. If this trend continues for another generation, it may very well be too late to regain the attention of masses of Black youth, instill into them more constructive values, and focus them on more productive pursuits.

The irony of rap is that all of the high-end materialistic possessions worshipped by the rap culture, including luxury automobiles, mansions, diamonds and gold, expensive travel, high-quality spirits, etc., are completely out of reach of the typical rap fan. Additionally, while rap glorifies materialism, it misses the point that someone had to get educated to develop all of these material goods. Someone had to become an architect to design the mansions, an automotive engineer to design the Bentleys, an aerospace engineer to build the airplane that takes you to Cancun, a gemologist to produce the "bling" diamonds, etc. So with some exceptions, rap's message is one of consumerism, in a time when Black's need producers more than ever before, particularly since a kid is extremely unlikely to grow up to become a successful entertainer or athlete. Rap would serve the Black community well if it channeled its messages to focus Black youth to pursue the more constructive disciplines required to produce the materialistic goods that their industry admires.

White Denial

The Final Ingredient

This racial illiteracy on the part of white people is part of the hegemonic power of whiteness. Through a historical mythology, white supremacy has a vested interest in denying what is most obvious: the privileged position of whiteness. For most people who are described as white, since race is believed to be "something" that shapes the lives of people of color, they often fail to recognize the ways in which their own lives and our public policies are shaped by race. Structural or institutionalized racism is not merely a matter of individual attitudes, but the result of centuries of subordination and objectification that reinforce population control policies.

–Loretta J. Ross,[22] Executive Director,
National Center for Human Rights

Let me be clear. There have always been many White Americans who have with passion, recognized the injustice, dehumanization, and peril of Black America. These Whites, from the beginning, jeopardized their own lives, families, and security, as they responded to their moral consciousness and took on antiestablishment roles in order to right the wrongs confronting humanity during their time.

During slavery, these Whites became abolitionists, operated Underground Railroad stops, helped slaves escape, and fought to change legislation to be fair and equitable. Many Whites during and postslavery taught Blacks to read and write, befriended Blacks, employed Blacks, partnered with, and in, some cases, even married African Americans.

There are sound-minded, right-hearted White Americans who have reached out to help and/or secure the livelihood of Blacks whom they have come to know, trust, and care for. In my own life, which came of age during the end of the civil rights movement, I can recount multiple instances of kind gestures toward me from Whites, which assured me that not all Whites are racists, which is a generalization that you grow up with in Black communities. In fact, my White associates have been more helpful to me in my life and career than Blacks have. Not just because they are more often in positions of influence, or that they feel "White guilt,"

[22.] Loretta J. Ross is the founder and executive director of the National Center for Human Rights Education, the USA partner of the Peoples' Decade of Human Rights Education.

but because they were "built" that way, simply fair-minded, kindhearted people.

It is my belief that a considerable percentage of America's "Black elite" are in their privileged position because they, or someone in their ancestry, had a good relationship with a White person who provided them with opportunity. Unfortunately, however, these Whites have historically been more of the exception than the rule. My life is much more littered with acts of rejection and disapproval by Whites than with kindness, understanding, and support.

As a general rule, White Americans have been at best impartial toward the Black plight in America and, at worst, downright hostile toward African Americans for no reason other than their skin color, subjecting them to sometimes subhuman treatment.

Particularly in the South, Whites generally believed in their hearts that Blacks were inferior creatures, worthy of nothing more than whatever Whites wished to subject them to at their whim. This hard-core belief of many Southern Whites was so strong that it overshadowed all other beliefs, religious or otherwise, and was not open to logic and reasoning.

Most Whites were Christians with a strong faith-based belief in the teachings of Jesus Christ. This is a key point of denial. For how can you follow the teachings of Jesus and live by the scriptures of the Bible and still treat people the way Blacks were treated? Even if Blacks were viewed as subhuman, good-hearted people would not treat any life form in a disrespectful and degrading way. Christianity, however, was no match for the conscious and subconscious ridicule and hatred that many Whites felt toward Blacks.

The irony is that particularly in the 1600s, 1700s, and 1800s, Blacks were almost completely humble and domicile. They had little or no means of independence and generally could not survive without the menial existence provided by slavery or bottom rung menial wage employment available to free Blacks. In other words, Blacks were completely powerless and at the mercy of White America. When you are in a clear and total position of power, and you completely hate, ridicule, and exploit those less fortunate, who have done absolutely nothing to deserve such wrath and, to the contrary, do everything to appease in order to avoid punishment, two possibilities emerge.

1. Those in power have a lack of moral character and are misguided human beings who don't care to see or understand how their obvious wrong-hearted behavior is affecting the lives of other families, or how their own children are being nurtured by this twisted evil perspective.
2. Those who are powerless lose all sense of self-esteem and worth, which starts to take root in their overall behavior and outlook on life, which, needless to say, gets absorbed by their children and their children's children.

Only the strongest willed members on each side can counteract the ill effects of such mental conditioning, particularly if exposed as young children.

White denial is clearly evidenced in a variety of recent events and positions taken on a variety of topics. In an earlier chapter, I recalled the Rodney King beating in 1991 by the Los Angeles Police Department (LAPD). Most Whites that I talked to supported the LAPD in their actions and did not understand the Black reaction to their acquittal verdict. Many would say that we don't know what happened before the beating was videotaped. I could not believe the complete state of denial in this statement as I pointed out to several Whites that it does not matter what you have done, once the police have you restrained, they are only supposed to arrest you, not beat you. Again, the example that I used, which usually worked, is when I reminded them of the event when John Hinckley shot President Ronald Reagan and James Brady, the police wrestled him to the ground then arrested him. They did not beat Hinckley, and he had just shot the president and a few others. The worst Rodney King did was to run a red light.

Other examples of White denial include the fact that until recent years, every police killing, shooting, or brutality event was against a person of color. While most of these instances were White on Black (or Hispanic), the police perpetrator was occasionally Black or Hispanic as well. The fact that the victims were almost always minorities is evidence of a social conditioning where African American lives are not seen as valuable or relevant by the authorities even when the representative of the authority (police) is an African American as well. I have personally witnessed Whites become offensive and belligerent toward a police officer who still treated that person with respect and almost deference. In a similar situation involving a Black, the Black is much more likely to experience the officer's wrath and potentially get arrested and thrown in jail. Keep in mind that the United States is still a majority White population. This means there are at least 175 million White people here. Statistically speaking, at least half of the police brutality incidents should be against White people. Barring the fact that Whites generally are better situated in life with decent jobs, functional families, etc., it still begs the question, why do Whites have very few recorded negative encounters with police officers?

More recently, however, Whites are encountering police brutality events themselves. Society is changing even where Whites are concerned. This was made clear in Chicago where a White off-duty police officer became upset at a bar when the female bartender, also White, refused to serve another drink because he had too much already. The policeman commenced to beating the small-framed lady, and it was all caught on video. To make matters worse, fellow officers tried to threaten and bribe the lady and the establishment, which was recorded as well. Incidents like this one reveal to White America what Blacks have been complaining about for decades. However, until police brutality, drugs, gangs, and shootings impact the White community, there is little reaction toward addressing the problems.

In recent polls that gauge the effect of race on jobs, opportunities, and education, Whites rate improved equality much more favorably than Blacks even though wealth, power, and influence are still almost completely wielded by Whites; and Blacks continue to be disproportionately poor, uneducated, and societal outcasts.

With the recent victory of President Barack Obama, it should be clear how much innate racism continues to exist. While Obama was able to capture a majority of the White vote, which, because of his color, would not have been possible in decades gone by, one of the most disturbing statistics against Obama had nothing to do with his character, platform, or political abilities, but was the fact that many Whites simply could not bring themselves to vote for a Black man. Some of these Whites were very successful, powerful, and influential people, and I personally talked to a dozen or more. Considering that many Whites who were confronted with the possibility of a Black president, and searched their souls to find that they could not vote for him, are in positions of influence, it does not take a genius to recognize that these otherwise well-intended folks have some deeply ingrained predispositions toward Blacks that likely affect their judgment toward other Blacks that they might encounter on a daily basis. How do their beliefs consciously or subconsciously affect their judgment about the Blacks they encounter when considering them for a job, a promotion, or some other responsibility of importance?

When considering the need for equal opportunities and affirmative action, Whites simply need to look around themselves. In most successful productive environments, they will see that there aren't many Blacks around, if any. Blacks are significantly absent from affluent middle-class neighborhoods, white-collar corporate environments, business travelers on airplanes, major sports events, social, golf and country club settings, boats docked at harbors, retirement communities, college campuses, youth camps, and other semblance of affluence. While at the same time Blacks are tremendously overrepresented in the country's prison system, poor communities, failing schools, dysfunctional families, uneducated and unemployed population, violent crimes, and negative social economic statistics.

A clear expression of White denial came when Michelle Obama, while campaigning for her husband, Barack, made the statement,

"For the first time in my adult life, I am really proud to be an American." Michelle Obama was expressing appreciation and gratitude that the United States of America has finally evolved beyond its purely race-based judgments and is moving past all of the negative realities toward Blacks presented in this book, and is actually considering a Black man as its leader and commander in chief. However, much of the White opposition in politics and in the media completely ignored the true meaning of her words and characterized her statements as those made by some sort of anti-American traitor and ridiculed her as being unpatriotic.

Another case is the comment that Senator Harry Reid made regarding Barack Obama's electability based on his being a "light skinned" African American who doesn't speak with a "Negro dialect." While I don't believe these statements make Senator Reid a racist, I do see him acknowledging White America's racist tendencies and see White denial inherent in his remarks in two ways:

1. Senator Reid obviously perceives that a darker African American cannot be elected, and that an African American who "sounds Black" cannot be elected. I agree with Senator Reid, but doesn't his statement reveal that something is wrong in our society? What are we doing to fix it?
2. Regarding the "Negro dialect" comment, doesn't Senator Reid know that this Negro dialect, which is spoken by many African Americans, is a dialect that evolved from hundreds of years of Blacks needing to speak in an inferior manner to survive in the United States of America? Are we saying that we know that this dialect, which was imposed on African Americans, is limiting their success in our great nation? What are we doing about that?

Many Whites do not seem to be connected to the history of the Black struggle even though much of it is fairly recent, and many Whites are relatively old people who lived through it. This condition appears to be the result of two primary factors:

1. Whites have primarily been responsible for the content of history books and the educational curriculum in which

history is taught. So the kaleidoscope of Black history and its effect on African Americans has never been a priority, and the full impact and contribution that Blacks have had on the formation and evolution of America, and the protection of its way of life, has been relatively ignored. So consequently, many Whites actually don't see or get the common Black perspective that Michelle Obama expressed earlier.

2. Whites generally do not make a connection between White skin and the privilege that White skin affords, since for them, White skin is completely normal, and they face struggles and challenges in their White skin every day. Furthermore, when Whites are in the middle and lower rungs of society and perceives that their starting position is no better than anyone else, including African Americans, they may not realize the universal acceptance of their Whiteness, allowing them to sometimes despise perceived preferences for minorities.

Bill O'Reilly, the talk show host of the O'Reilly Factor, had a show where he expressed to an African American guest that Bill's upbringing was no different than that of many African Americans in the country, yet he was able to overcome meager beginnings and excel to heights not common among the environment from which he came. O'Reilly clearly does not understand the privilege that his Whiteness has afforded him, especially in his generation where many of the prejudices and preconceived notions about African American would have been common in most folks' minds since O'Reilly came of age during the heat of the civil rights movement. It is interesting that O'Reilly, obviously an intelligent man, cannot associate all of the negative noise regarding Black people that he must have been exposed to while growing up and in young adulthood, with the plausibility that many Black people were being adversely affected by the general sentiment that created and harbored those negative perceptions. All you have to do is connect the dots. Whites are the majority, Whites have the power, influence, and money, many Whites have a bad attitude toward Blacks, Blacks are the minority, and Blacks do not have much power, influence, or money. Who is likely to be disadvantaged in this scenario?

Another denial case occurred on the Oprah Winfrey show when one of her guests was Charles Murray, coauthor of the controversial book *The Bell Curve*. During the question-and-answer period where Oprah gave her audience an opportunity to directly address questions and comments to Murray, a young Black man commented on the fact that in general, when out shopping in a mall or other public arena, White people, particularly middle-aged White women, but others as well, tense up and make gestures to protect their purse and other belongings when they realize any Black male is in their presence. Murray then commented that what the young man described is a reasonable reaction by White people when around Black men. Murray was implying that since Black men have a high incarceration rate and are disproportionately represented in prison and the criminal population, it is reasonable to conclude that the Black man you are observing while shopping is likely to be a criminal and have criminal intent. What Murray fails to recognize is that this perspective that he thinks is reasonable is actually racist, as it generalizes Black males. Fewer Whites, and most other people correctly evaluate the Black male more closely to assess his likely character, social status and affluence before simply assuming he is a threat simply based on his black skin.

The kind of generalization that Murray promoted is just as unreasonable as the following hypothetical scenarios that can be reasoned using the same logic that Murray applies to the assessment of Black men in your presence:

- It is reasonable for a woman alone in an elevator or other public place to perceive that she is in danger of rape whenever a male is present since 99 percent of rape is conducted by men (mostly White)
- It is reasonable for minorities to assume that all White people are racist since most racist acts in the United States has been carried out by White people
- We should perceive that all people of German decent are Nazis since most Nazis were people of German decent
- We should perceive that the White man standing near you is likely to be a serial killer since serial killers are disproportionately White males

- It is reasonable to assume that the White male management at your employer is calculating how to rip the company off via "White collar crime" and steal your retirement benefits since corporate rip-offs to date are always executed by White men

Other examples of unreasonable conclusions drawn by some White perspectives include as follows:

- Whites sometimes protest when Blacks with lower standard test scores are admitted into a college or university ahead of them while ignoring the admittance of many Whites who also achieved lower test scores than they did
- Thousands of Whites questioned the legitimacy of Barack Obama's presidency and demanded proof of citizenship via his birth certificate when White president's birthplace legitimacy is never questioned
- The media, institutions, and public safety organizations consistently ignore the thousands of Black youth who are killed, abused, or missing each year, which undermines the value of these lives and condones a reality that should be recognized as an outrageous national crisis
- Black youths arrested for drug possession for the first time are incarcerated at a rate that is *forty-eight times greater* than the rate for White youth even when all other factors surrounding the crime are equal
- Job applicants with "White sounding" names, according to a University of Chicago study, are 50 percent more likely to be called for a job interview than those with "Black sounding" names even when all of their credentials are similar
- Black males are three times more likely than White males to have their vehicles stopped and searched by police even though White males are over four times more likely to posses illegal contraband on the occasions when they are searched

White denial is not a new phenomenon brought on by the mass media psychosocial manipulation discussed earlier, but has been a part of White society in the United States since the introduction of slavery hundreds of years ago. Consider this excerpt from history:

- Dr. Samuel Cartwright, a well-respected physician of the nineteenth century, named a disease to explain the tendency of many slaves to run away. He called it Drapetomania: an affliction that could be cured by keeping the slave in an intimidated "child-like state" and ensuring not to treat them as equals while yet striving not to be too cruel. "Whipping the devil out of them" was, to Cartwright, the best cure of all. In Dr. Cartwright's eyes, not only was enslavement and racial oppression not the issue; but those Blacks who resisted it, or refused to bend to it, or complained about it, were to be viewed as mentally ill.[23]

Even during the tumultuous 1960s, when racial oppression was nationally recognized and at an all-time high, Whites had a propensity to underestimate the ravaging effects that racism and oppression had on Black communities and individuals. Consider these Newsweek/Gallup poll results:

- In 1963, before the passage of meaningful civil rights legislation, two-thirds of Whites said that they believed Blacks were treated the same as Whites in their communities.[24]
- In 1962, eighty-five percent of Whites said Black children had just as good a chance as White children to get a good education in their communities.[25]
- In 1968, seventy percent of Whites said that Blacks were treated the same as Whites in their communities.[26]

[23.] Cartwright, Samuel. 1851. "Diseases and Peculiarities of the Negro Race," *DeBow's Review*. (Southern and Western States: New Orleans), Vol. XI.

[24.] The Gallup Organization, Gallup Poll Social Audit, 2001. Black-White Relations in the United States, 2001 Update, July 10: 7-9.

[25.] The Gallup Organization, Gallup Poll Social Audit, 2001. Black-White Relations in the United States, 2001 Update, July 10: 7-9

[26.] The Gallup Organization, Gallup Poll Social Audit, 2001. Black-White Relations in the United States, 2001 Update, July 10: 7-9

- In 1963, three-fourths of White Americans told Newsweek, "The Negro is moving too fast" in his demands for equality.[27]
- in 1964, two-thirds of Whites said that the Civil Rights Act should be enforced gradually, with an emphasis on persuading employers not to discriminate, as opposed to forcing compliance with equal opportunity requirements.[28]
- In 1969, forty-four percent of Whites told a Newsweek/Gallup National Opinion Survey that Blacks had a better chance than they did to get a good paying job, and forty-two percent said Blacks had a better chance for a good education than Whites.[29]

Finally, in a recent study by the University of Chicago on the handling of the Hurricane Katrina catastrophe by the U.S. government in New Orleans, a current state of White denial can be evidenced. The study asked if you believed the Katrina tragedy showed that there was a lesson to be learned about racial inequality in America. Only 38 percent of Whites agreed. Even as Blacks were disproportionately affected in terms of who was stuck in New Orleans, who was able to escape, who has been able to return, and whose property was condemned to make way for commercial uses.[30]

The mass media psychosocial program described earlier perpetuates a depiction of Black people that is a profoundly distorted view that elevates the ailments of Black America above all that is good and right with Black America. Its portrayal of Black America ignores all facts that conflict with racist conceptions and sees the problems of Black America as rooted primarily with

---

[27] "How Whites Feel About Negroes: A Painful American Dilemma," *Newsweek*, October 21, 1963: 56

[28] The Gallup Organization, Gallup Poll #699, October, 1964

[29] Newsweek/Gallup Organization, National Opinion Survey, August 19, 1969

[30] Ford, Glen and Peter Campbell, 2006. "Katrina: A Study-Black Consensus, White Dispute," The Black Commentator, Issue 165, January 5

Blacks themselves, instead of emanating from a legacy of White racism and oppression from slavery to today. This program revises the past and conveniently makes Whites appear less inhumane throughout America's brutal racist past. Despite a brutal history to the contrary, mass media fraudulently depicts Whites as being the standard of ethics and moral values while portraying Blacks as being all that's wrong with America and the catalyst to America's downward social and moral decline. The mass media program also facilitates a national consensual environment where Blacks' cries for equality are ignored and their mistreatment becomes justifiably tolerable. While this mass media psychosocial program has been less blatant than those earlier racist systems used against Blacks in the past, its effects are, in general, very real and detrimental. In fact, this mass media manipulation of perceptions and beliefs is the engine that enables White denial and is, by far, the most proficient system of control to ever be deployed against America's Black population.

While working with a friend who happens to be a venture capitalist on a prospective business idea that I would lead, I asked him about his observation in corporate boardrooms of the perception of White corporate executives toward Black-run businesses. He honestly stated that the general consensus would be that Black-run businesses are incompetent and not worthy of consideration. He did not necessarily agree with that position, which is why we were talking to begin with, and pointed out to me, in his state of White denial, that there are racist Blacks just as there are racist Whites. However, he easily saw my counterpoint that while there are racist Blacks, Blacks have no significant capital, power, or influence. In fact, he had participated in venture capital conferences all around the country for a decade and could count the number of Black venture capitalists that he had met on one hand. Successful Blacks are few and far in between when it comes to money, power, and influence. White denial had my good friend blind to that reality.

During George W. Bush's eight years of presidency, he was frequently made fun of by the media because of his intellectual fumbles, inarticulate comments, and usual mix-up of words, countries, or organizations. The media and White population treated President Bush's slipups and indications of lack of knowledge almost as if it was cute and endearing. Everything from how he got into Yale and Harvard, to his academic performance while he was there, to his military status and contributions, were seemingly the sole result of privilege rather than individual merit. White America would have taken a completely different and negative position had President Bush been Black. Every word that he spoke would have been scrutinized and judged and served to confirm his inferior human status in the eyes of many Whites. But since President Bush is White, then he's all right.

Many times in my own career experience, I have been told by Whites that the only reason I am in my position is because I am Black, as if I could not possibly be qualified or good at what I do. In one instance, a White colleague suggested to me that if he and I were interviewing for a job where we were equally qualified, that I would get the job because I am Black and that is unfair to him. I swiftly pointed out and he conceded that if I did get the job because I am Black, it is because there are already five hundred White guys there due to past racial discrimination.

White denial enables Whites to be blind to such offenses as naming sport team mascots after people or groups (i.e., Chief Illini or the Red Skins). Even as the offended group expresses discomfort with the association, many Whites essentially ignore the offended as if they are overreacting and unreasonable. White denial prevents Whites from recognizing and acknowledging the fact that the majority of people imprisoned for criminal activity, especially drug related, are African American, when it is common for White people to know someone White involved with drugs but without a criminal record. Simple statistical analysis would strongly indicate a problem based on a White majority population. In my own community, which is one of the most affluent communities in the country, there are regular occurrences of drug abuse among youth and adults. In many cases involving high school youths, there is public service intervention designed to correct the behavior of the youth outside of the judicial system. Where I went to high school, and in most urban ghettos, the youth goes directly to jail. In addition, the occasional drug abuse among many professional adults in this affluent community is an indicator that in less-affluent middle—and lower-middle class White communities, drug abuse is rampant. However, no one is closely watching the White drug abusers; therefore, they are severely underrepresented in our judicial system.

If you can't see, acknowledge, or understand the problem, then you might be a part of it. White denial may be the most enabling factor of oppression in the plight of Blacks in America since the inability to empathize prevents people from perceiving reality from another's point of view. As a result, many Whites are desensitized to the concerns and challenges of the disadvantaged and incorrectly perceive that opportunities are equally available to African Americans as to themselves, when in fact, the African American has more challenges with each opportunity that Whites typically do not endure. As a result, many Whites perceive Blacks as incompetent or inadequate in many ways, and when Blacks genuinely achieve stature or position, many Whites attribute the Black's success as being purely the result of their minority status rather than their character and ability.

One outcome of White denial is rendered in any technology field. It becomes clear that the American society has had an ill effect on the education and welfare of its African American citizens. You only need to look around the technology arena at the disproportionate number of highly skilled, highly paid immigrant workers and realize that many of these positions could have been filled from within the population of millions of Black U.S. citizens already here. But due to systematic neglect and oppression over hundreds of years, and discriminatory practices over recent decades, African Americans are left ill-equipped to qualify for or respond to many of the best jobs that our nation has to offer. As a result, the United States imports hundreds of thousands of technology workers from India, China, Europe, and other parts of the world. Now don't get me wrong. I have many friends and colleagues among the ranks of these foreign employees; however, I can't help but feel sorrow, thinking about the many African American men and women who are already here and could have been equally educated, trained, and skilled in many of the disciplines that we now import people for while still neglecting the schools and communities in predominantly African American areas. We bring in hundreds of thousands of foreigners, who may or may not have the best interest of America at heart, while our very own citizens continue to wallow in despair. But rather than correct the societal ills that have rendered African Americans ill-equipped to fill this void in our workplace, we take the shortsighted approach.

The simple fact that virtually all of the United States companies, organizations, and institutions are controlled and operated by Whites, and that Whites have a monopoly on money, power, and influence, leads you to conclude that unless these Whites in high places know and are friendly with qualified Blacks who they like, interact with, and potentially support and mentor into these organizations, then it is unlikely that many Blacks make it into these wealth-building relationships and organizations since people extend opportunities to people who they know, like, and are comfortable with, and those are normally people who are similar to themselves.

If African Americans had been provided fair treatment since slavery—in housing, education, employment and business opportunities—it is plain to see that millions more would have achieved educational levels beneficial to society. Not only would the quality of service rendered by African Americans today be improved wherever they work, but millions of underproductive African Americans would be better qualified to work in many other capacities. You can argue that a better educated and more productive Black population would have resulted in tens of thousands of American lives saved, and tens of billions of dollars saved or created over the past century. This would have been the effect from a greater productivity factor and improved intellectual capacity in all facets of American society, public and private. Consider Dr. Ben Carson[31] as a sample of the untapped potential in the Black community.

---

[31] Dr. Benjamin S. Carson, MD, born September 18, 1951, in Detroit Michigan, is a neurosurgeon and the director of Pediatric Neurosurgery at Johns Hopkins Hospital. Dr. Carson was raised by an impoverished

If currently successful Blacks are any indication of the untapped human potential that lies in this dedicated and loyal but marginalized and dysfunctional segment of our society, then America has really done itself a disservice by holding a "blind eye" to possibilities that existed and by not recognizing the error in the flawed relationship with its African American citizens.

While many Blacks have achieved varying degrees of prominence in business, education, government, and other fields, race remains one of the most intractable problems in the United States. This is because personal biases and racial stereotyping cannot be altered by legislation or legal action. This lingering prejudice toward African Americans, combined with a subliminal sense of white superiority and entitlement, fosters a perpetual state of White denial that forms the largest obstacle to reconciling and healing our society's blighted racial past and moving forward toward an all-inclusive, harmonious future in our country.

---

mother who could not read, and he initially did not show promise as a student.

Summary

African American Re-reconstruction

The fractured and sometimes nonexistent integrity in the lineage of African Americans makes it impossible for the African American to be judged by the same standard as White America because for hundreds of years, the African American has had a legacy of dysfunction passed down as its heritage, crippling one generation after another, resulting in a race that is largely damaged and dysfunctional today.

For more than four hundred years, the United States government created and supported an environment that rendered African Americans victimized and debilitated, leaving their members socially, economically, and psychologically bankrupt. This occurred in the greatest country on earth during the world's greatest period of prosperity from industrial, technological, and economic advancement. During this time, great episodes of American history have played out producing powerful lucrative industries such as agriculture, housing, apparel, transportation (rail, auto, and air), steel, construction, publishing, telecommunications, health care, financial services, computing technology, and more.

While African Americans have lived in the United States this entire time, they have had only a miniscule participation, if any, in the formation, development, and ownership of the companies, organizations, and institutions of which these industries are comprised. As a result of African American's inability to participate in the development of these corporate organizations from individual embryonic entities into international conglomerates, the African American community is left largely impotent and substantially lacking a robust widespread socioeconomic means of self-determination, wealth creation, pride and human capital development.

As stated earlier, you can reason only one of two causes for this four-hundred-year-old reality. Either, African Americans are inherently inferior and have lacked the ability to constructively innovate and engineer ways to produce and deliver products and services into the marketplace thereby creating progressive communities and wealth, or, the marketplace has historically been off-limits to African Americans and has severely constrained their ability to participate in any meaningful way by simply denying them access to education, good jobs, capital, services, partners, and customers. Based on overwhelming evidence presented by history in support of discriminatory constraints against African Americans, and no concrete evidence to the contrary, this book concludes that African Americans have been systematically shut out of the opportunities created by the wonderful economic engine of the United States of America while the United States government neglectfully contributed to the dysfunction and despair apparent in the Black community to this day. This is not to say that the United States government has done nothing to promote the advancement of African Americans, but that its corrective actions have been anemic when compared to the need to repair damage done to a population of citizens actually created in the United States of America.

Furthermore, the U.S. government's actions tended to be "quick-fixes" designed to accommodate the en vogue self-interest of the country's White majority, rather than the proactive healing of the badly damaged soul and condition of the nation and a group of its people. Hence the Emancipation Proclamation, the Freedmen's Bureau, civil rights legislation, attempts at bussing, affirmative action, racial quotas, welfare, and other remedies were all conceived during times of social and political unrest; but as the unrest subsided, so did the energy behind the change. In most cases as the unrest settled, so did any significant interest in the equalization of African Americans, once again leaving them socially and economically ill-equipped to make meaningful inroads into the mainstream of this great capitalistic system.

To honestly consider the cause and effect of the African American condition and the magnitude of the disparity and prejudice that existed over time, you have to be willing to recognize that your current perceptions and belief system regarding African Americans has been tampered with. African Americans have never possessed controlling interest in any of the major media institutions, industries, and organizations of the United States. While recent positive progress is being made, these communications entities have historically created, managed, monitored, and presented African American imagery in very self-serving ways, which have perpetuated negative stereotypical views of African Americans, particularly Black males. This has been evidenced in the news and entertainment media for generations, where the predominant image presented of African Americans was one of crime, poverty, despair, sex, guns, violence, and other negative social ills. This long-lasting perpetuation of negative imagery regarding African Americans was a major detrimental factor in the plight of African Americans in recent times. The pervasive bombardment of these images over the communications media within the United States for decades of time and generations of people created a belief system that is not based on factual information and statistics, but rather the persuasive selling of ideas and perceptions influenced by the interest of the controlling parties.

For years since the advent of motion pictures and television, you could rarely find a Black person presented in a dignified and respectful manner to the millions of people in the American population. While at the same time, the standards for White images were predominantly productive, constructive, and good. The media shapes and reflects the views and opinions of the nation. As such, many people—Black, White, and others—are influenced by the repetitive nature of stereotypical imagery broadcasted and published. Since all of American government and industry has been historically controlled by White America, and White America's perception of African Americans has been historically adversely impacted by the media, it's easy to conclude that meaningful opportunities for African Americans in government and industry have been limited guided by the conscious or subconscious thoughts of Whites. People are not likely to place individuals whom they believe (consciously or subconsciously) are inherently dysfunctional, incompetent, or criminal into positions of responsibility or authority. People are also not likely to live around individuals whom they perceive are inherently dangerous or criminal. Black people are themselves likely to feel hopeless and marginalized when they perceive themselves as outcasts of society and not fitting of mainstream social and economic graces. While these perceptions were largely manufactured, these are real and current perceptions of African Americans by Whites, African Americans, and a growing number of other nationalities exposed to the current African American condition. As a result, the perceptions feed reality, making Black marginalization a self-fulfilling prophecy, particularly as many Blacks themselves internalize and believe the dysfunctional stereotypical perceptions, and then acting on their belief system consequently making them reality.

Since the 1970s, the United States has been growing increasingly diversified and more open to racial and ethnic diversity. This phenomenon has been termed "the browning of America" as Hispanics, Indians, Middle Easterners, Asians, and others have been immigrating to the United States in ever-growing numbers. While America's growing acceptance of its minority population has been a well-deserved outcome won largely through the pain and suffering of African Americans, the African American is still largely unaccepted by mainstream America due to the preconditioned mind-sets described earlier. A Jewish friend of mine who owns his own company employing around four hundred people shared his perception with me that in his organization, every minority hire is easily accepted into the "fabric" of his company except the African American. He had no explanation other than "that's just the way it is."

While some of these sentiments have merit due to the fact that many African Americans are dysfunctional today, the larger issue is the generalized preconceived notions that many have about Blacks regardless of the individual merit and character that educated or otherwise qualified Blacks bring to the table.

There is a significant number of African Americans who, through the grace of God or just sheer luck, emerged from our withered past as educated, dynamic, well-rounded, articulate, and talented individuals. Many of these individual's full potential, however, may never be realized since their paths are unlikely to coincide with powerful and influential White people who not only takes an interest in the talented Black person but brings him/her along as well. And as most people know, more times than not, opportunity does not only result from what you know, but more importantly, from who you know. And since Whites control the power, influence, and money in the United States of America, they are the primary gatekeepers of who is allowed to excel.

The worst part of America's newly found acceptance of minority participation in America's mainstream is the fact that the unprepared African American is being left out and replaced by workers from other nations in productive and meaningful occupations. Due to the oppressive history described earlier and the self-defeating behavior that ultimately resulted from hopelessness and despair, millions of Blacks are now simply cast aside as not useful to society. As the need expands for highly skilled knowledge workers and those with skills in various technology areas, the United States is importing hundreds of thousands of workers to fill well-paying jobs here in America.

Now that the country has a growing demand for "knowledge workers," the African American, who has been here from the beginning—but neglected and largely uneducated—is substantially incapable of fulfilling the workplace demands of the country. Had the United States been more accepting, protective, interested, and vested in its African American citizens over the past few hundred years, one can only imagine how competitive the United States would be today. If you consider the progress of Blacks who have broken through the racial barriers in America and the tremendous contributions that they have made, just think of how greater a nation we may have become if the United States had actually cultivated its Black population instead of trampling it over the years. It's not too late. But we have to begin acknowledging the root cause of the issues, accept responsibility for their origins, and craft a reasonable solution as a, once and for all, reconciliation of past treatment designed as an earnest attempt to heal a broken people.

Reconstruction Now or Never

Since the United States' current economic crisis is challenging with its growing debt and budget deficits, the country might need to re-evaluate the tens of billions of dollars that it administers in foreign aid every year and begin to focus priority on improving it's own people and internal challenges. You are always in a better position to help others when you take care of yourself first. As such, reconstruction for African Americans should be considered now before it is too late and the following factors take hold.

Antireparation spokespeople claim that too much time has passed, and there is no way to identify people who have been directly affected or are the descendants of those directly affected by the oppressive elements of American society. The naysayers believe that America has become too complicated, progressive, and diversified, and that its people are more righteous, inclusive, and interracially mixed. They say that there cannot be a fair and accurate way to structure reparations in a way that it targets those intended.

There are continuing claims about how other folks in society such as European immigrants, Hispanics, and Asians are making it without any special consideration. In addition, as time passes, more and more Americans reach age of majority as upstanding, law-abiding, voting citizens; and many of them, from all ethnic groups, have lost touch with the history and the struggle of African Americans that persisted over four hundred years. These youthful Americans, generally born after 1970, were not exposed to the nationally broadcasted episodes of the civil rights movement where Blacks were regularly beaten, gassed, dog attacked, fire hosed, and otherwise mistreated in their pursuit of a seat at the local diner or anywhere on a bus or in society.

If it has not occurred already, it will not be long before a new generation of Americans simply views Black America as victims of themselves rather than victims of an unjust society. The reality is that Black America has been left socially, economically, spiritually, politically, and educationally castrated by the deeply penetrating ill effects of hundreds of years of slavery and oppression in a White-dominated society.

The position that reconstruction be considered now before it is too late is directly related to two evolving factors of the American population:

1. Those born in the 1970s or later have no experience or memory of the regularly overt and publicized events that clearly revealed racial issues in society resulting in African American oppression
2. There is an enormous wave of immigrants who have arrived in the United States since the 1960s, are changing the profile of our nation, and have no vested interest in America's past, or in remedies for African Americans.

Time is quickly moving forward and closing the chapter on the Black experience in America. While there will always be historical references to these events, society will eventually view it as just that, historical references to these events. Time has a way of lessening the pain, smoothing out the edges, losing touch with the details, making things less Black and White and more gray. This of course happens as society evolves. People die, connections to the past are lost, new issues or crisis emerge, migrations happen, sentiment changes, politics and philosophies evolve, the next thing you know, the factors that support reconstruction are just historical references to past events rather than a debt owed by society.

However, today we have many people alive who remember the horror of overt racism, many social conditions that can be directly connected to oppression uncontested, a general sentiment in society for fairness and to do the right thing, and a new generation of people who, if made consciously aware of the factors causing the Black condition, would probably recognize and support the notion of reconstruction if common-sense solutions can be brought forward. However, if we become one or two more generations removed from direct connections to our blighted past through people, or the knowledge that an unjust society originated most of the ills suffered In Black communities, it will become difficult to continue the discussion of reconstruction let alone actually achieve it.

Many fear that reparations to African Americans mean a substantial cash payout to everyone who claims to be of African descent in America. While this is an obvious option, it is by far the least sensible and practical. In fact, "well off" African Americans may receive no benefit at all. We must explore ideas where society can offset hundreds of years of oppression and aim to relieve some of the fundamental flaws in the Black community. In addition, reconstruction remedies should be made available to any American in need but be concentrated in those poverty-stricken communities with large African American populations where the results of oppression appear most evident. An approach like this will support the fact that there are varying degrees of the impact of past racial discrimination on African Americans. It acknowledges that it would be difficult to identify who actually should benefit from reconstruction and will attempt to accommodate these variances in its application.

Reconstruction programs would be designed to instill self-worth and respect in individuals, a sense of purpose and future possibilities for their lives, community involvement, academic and vocational skill development, and a connection to mainstream opportunities, among other benefits.

A Plausible Reconstruction Solution

I do not advocate administering sums of money to people who are proven to be descendants of slavery or affected by racism, discrimination, and oppression. I think any program that distributes money to individuals must have clear criteria, guidelines, and controls, and this would be difficult to accomplish at best where the African American problem is concerned, due to their extremely fractured and fragmented past. I would propose programs that would fundamentally contribute structurally to the foundation of African American communities and strengthens the people and their social and economic stability by remedying the following ailments:

- Racial discrimination effects
- Community degradation
- Disruption of family life
- Educational degradation
- Arbitrary deprivation of liberty
- Pain and suffering
- Disruption of mental, physical and spiritual health
- Loss of cultural rights and fulfillment
- Labor exploitation
- Economic loss
- Opportunity loss

The various programs would be designed to infuse self-esteem and responsibility through education (academic, health, physical, nutritional, and financial), community pride, child care, drug and alcohol abuse prevention, social skills, job training, vocational and trade skills, career and financial goals, and more. The programs would structure a well-rounded communal "cocoon" to provide the support services needed to transform at least one entire generation of children into constructive, productive, upwardly mobile citizens. The objective would be to create a "controlled environment" that would protect the interest and development of the children in a revolutionary way, requiring the complete trust, buy in and commitment of the parents or guardian. The programs would intercept children at an optimum age for maximum probability of success and control their entire development process (mental, physical, emotional, social, spiritual and academic) until they reach the age of majority.

A federally appointed Commission on African American Reconstruction would be erected to draft a Reconstruction program to provide a variety of benefits to largely but not exclusively African American communities and may include, but would not be limited to the following:

1. Acknowledgement and Apology
   The United States president and each state's governor (where relevant—tbd)
   - Officially acknowledge the responsibility of their predecessors for the laws, policies, and practices that enabled the discrimination and oppression of African American people
   - Negotiate with the NAACP a form of words for official apologies to African American individuals, families, and communities and extend those apologies with wide and culturally appropriate publicity

2. National Reconstruction Fund
   - The United States government to appoint a board to establish and administer a National Reconstruction Fund.
   - The board to be constituted by African American and non-African Americans appointed in consultation with the NAACP in each state having substantial (TBD) populations of African Americans. That the majority of members to be African American and the board to be chaired by an African American born before 1960.
   - Ideas for funding should be explored to estimate the burden that should be borne by the U.S. government and a possible contribution ratio (i.e., 100:1) borne by the African American community and possibly the U.S. population at large on a voluntary basis

3. Mental Rehabilitation—measures to improve the individual's self-esteem and enhance the perception of his or her overall worth and vision for themselves

4. Socioeconomic Reformation—measures to improve the health and life expectancy, literacy, employment, and wealth of individuals, families, and communities

5. Social Justice
   - Mass media assessments to qualify the media's historically disruptive effect on African Americans and how American society has been "brainwashed" to negatively perceive African Americans
   - Mass media recalibration to identify aggressive practices for offsetting negative imagery and messaging toward African Americans and begin to neutralize and improve the perceptions of African Americans with productive roles in society
   - Increase the role of the private sector in the local economies, enhancing job creation and improving economic growth
   - Develop effective, accessible legal aid to decide allegations of human rights abuses, or abuses of government authorities
   - Intervene with alternative methods for handling juveniles
   - Assist in the empowerment of citizens, working through civic and economic organizations to ensure broader participation in political, cultural, social, and economic life

6. Education
   - The state governments to ensure that primary and secondary school curricula include substantial compulsory modules on African American history
   - All professionals who work with the Reconstruction effort's children, families, and communities to receive training about the history and effects of slavery, discrimination, and oppression

- All undergraduates and trainees in relevant professions (psychology, sociology, medicine, etc.) are to receive, as part of their core curriculum, education about the history and effects of slavery, discrimination, and oppression

7. Training and Development
   - Job skills
   - Professional skills
   - Vocational skills
   - Education counseling
   - Academic support
   - Career counseling
   - Leadership

8. Community Support Services
   - Community development
   - Child care
   - Parenting skills
   - Money management
   - Nutrition education
   - Youth Skills: peer pressure, conflict resolution, etc.
   - Boys and girls clubs
   - Role models, mentors

9. Lineage identification
   Genealogy research support will be made available for those interested to instill the sense of pride that can only come from familiarity with one's heritage, which the African American population is severely deficient.
   - Family history research and lineage tracing
   - Engage the service of experts to provision genealogical information regarding countries of origin
   - Training of African Americans as researchers, archivists, genealogists, and counselors to further enrich history

10. Recording of testimonies
    Record, preserve, and administer access to the testimonies of African Americans born before 1964, starting with the eldest members first, who wish to provide their history

in audio, audiovisual, or written form. The purpose is to capture undocumented historical accounts of experiences and observations that can be made available for research, literature, and educational purposes

There would be enforced criteria for access to and retention of these services and strict measurements to monitor and improve results. There would be an extreme focus on the development, education, security, and welfare of the children so that the next generation would have access to the kind of emotional confidence, stability, and nurturing that leads to feeling secure, smart, and purposeful. These programs would be hubbed in the heart of African American communities that are most distressed.

The programs would need to be structured so that they provide a real safety net for people who are truly on the fringe and can't pull themselves up since it is frequently very difficult and impractical in these communities for most people to overcome their economic and environmental ailments, let alone become functional enough to accomplish success.

Poor economics alone is destroying thousands of lives; since many parents can't afford proper child care or schooling, their children are subsequently exposed to the negative elements in the community and have no guidance or supervision during vulnerable periods of childhood development. In addition, Blacks generally have a shorter life span due to lack of basic nutrition and health knowledge and access to better quality food products. African Americans are more prone to credit problems and are more likely to be victims of fraudulent financial scams and high-risk debt because of limited knowledge about money and finances. Black children are rarely exposed to professional and upwardly mobile role models since the majority of working adults in the Black community have not achieved a level of employment that represent the best career choices that America has to offer.

Finally, there is a fundamental array of personal development and exposure to a variety of mainstream career opportunities that can help children develop a better vision of possibilities for their future. All of these concepts can be designed into a comprehensive set of public services to be administrated through these reconstruction efforts.

How Long Should Reconstruction Last?

Reconstruction would have to be a serious attempt to lift as many African Americans as possible into the American mainstream and would need to be supported long enough to fully impact the coming of age of at least one entire generation of African Americans.

I estimate that a period of fifty years of dedicated reconstruction activity would be required to repair some of the damage done to Blacks over the past four hundred years and produce a substantial turnaround in the lives and communities of the African American population most at risk. Keep in mind that reconstruction is not an attempt to "even the playing field" between Whites and Blacks. At this point, that can never be accomplished since great episodes of American history have already played out producing major industries such as agriculture, construction, transportation (auto, rail, air), steel, publishing, telecommunications, medicine, and computer technology to name a few. Reconstruction would simply be an attempt to improve the lives of a disproportionate number of African Americans who continue to be on a socioeconomic bottom without the consciousness, resources, or skills needed to uplift themselves or their community. Reconstruction would aim to break the chain of dysfunction, poverty, and despair and give future generations of millions of Blacks a shot at becoming productive, economically viable contributors to society.

When you consider the time line of the African American experience from the time the first African slave was brought to the shores of the United States through nearly three hundred years of slavery to one hundred years of discriminatory oppression and ending with fifty years of institutionalized injustice and inequality, you realize that in over four hundred years, over twenty generations of African Americans have been subjected to an environment that left all but the luckiest of them socially, economically, and psychically bankrupt in ways that are unimaginable by people who have not gone through such experiences.

No other people known to modern man has been stripped of their name, religion, identity, family ancestry, culture, property, pride, and dignity the way that the African American has in the United States of America. Even Black Africans in South Africa, during the time of apartheid, maintained a sense of pride and dignity in the knowledge of their heritage. With African Americans, the essence of being a human being and the most precious element of self to be extracted from a man was accomplished while under the jurisdiction of the U.S. government. The United States of America destroyed the self-esteem of the African American, leaving him/her very little to be organically proud of. And not only that, but the oppressive effects in the American society instilled into generations of African Americans, a belief system that mirrors the negative perceptions that were largely manufactured by the White majority. These internalized dysfunctional and destructive beliefs are deeply entrenched into the culture and identity of many African Americans today. To undo the stereotyped "brain washing," character assassination, and arrested development inflicted on nearly an entire race of people, solutions with equal intensity must be applied to the root causes and need to be administered over a duration of time long enough to reverse the patterns. The targeted and focused development of at least one or two generations of African Americans will be required to accelerate healing the socioeconomic, health, and psychic damage done to the group and begin to equalize a critical mass of African Americans rendering them more productive.

U.S. Reconstruction Precedents

- U.S. Guarantees to American Indians
- U.S. Reparations to Japanese Americans
- U.S. Aid to Post WWII Europe
- Post-World War II Assistance to Germany
- Post-World War II Assistance to Japan
- U.S. Aid to Israel
- U.S. Aid to IRAQ
- U.S. Aid to Afghanistan

There are several precedents where the United States acknowledged harm done to groups of people or nations and provided restitution, support, and goodwill to support their recovery. Why then should not the United States consider harm done to its African American population and determine the appropriate level of reconstruction required to at least improve this group's condition and long-term viability, if not correct for past harm? Meaningful restitution for this group, who again, are the only Americans actually created in the United States, would not only be fair, but considering the contributions of this group, and the opportunity loss this group has suffered while in the greatest country on earth during the past four hundred years, it would also be the right thing to do.

U.S. Guarantees to American Indians

Let's be clear, the treatment of Native American Indians by the United States of America is an atrocity that almost made extinct the original owners of this land. The American Indian was used, abused, pushed aside, and nearly exterminated·before the country settled on the solution of Indian reservations. While this four-hundred-year history is despicable as well, American Indian survivors—while severely crippled politically, socioeconomically, and in other ways—at least retained a connection to a rich heritage, culture, language, rituals, and the like that can be a source of ethnic pride today. In addition, American Indians are the only minorities mentioned by name in the Constitution as Congress made treaties with the tribes that guaranteed health care, education, housing, and an entire range of services. American Indian entitlements are contractual agreements based on historical treaties.

In the early 1800s, the U.S. government set aside over 150 million acres of land and created Native American reservations. The Indian tribes were free to live as they wished on their lands, as long as they remained peaceful. Many reservations were located away from the major routes of White commerce, which, in some cases, inadvertently provided some tribes with an endowment in energy resources. Some reservations in Western states include rich deposits of coal, natural gas, uranium, and oil. While Native American Indians were surely taken advantage of in all aspects of human infringement, the land that was granted to American Indians over a century ago is starting to pay dividends. In addition to possessing tax-free property, many reservations have the ability to establish gaming casinos and are rewarded with magnificently high-profit margins. While much of the reservation land was, at the time, undesirable from a commercial and farming perspective, it is growing in appeal to wildlife enthusiast, nature lovers, adventurers, hunters, and fishermen. Many of these virtually untouched parcels of land are beginning to offer commercial opportunities that can be exploited by the Native American population for generations to come. I would expect that each new generation of American Indians will become more mainstream as a result of their emerging economic opportunities and the privileges it will enable.

U.S. Reparations to Japanese Americans

Japanese Americans also have suffered deprivations of civil rights, since at least the late nineteenth century. Asians faced low immigration quotas before the laws were amended in 1965, 1968, and 1977; and in certain regions of the United States, Asian Americans have been denied equal rights in housing and employment. Many Japanese Americans lost their property and livelihood while confined in internment camps during World War II. The forced removal and incarceration of persons of Japanese descent from the West Coast during World War II (1939-1945), which was upheld by the Supreme Court, was a major violation of civil liberties for which Congress apologized and began providing reparations in 1968, two decades after the internment camps were closed, for property they had lost.

In 1980, the U.S. Congress created the Commission on Wartime Relocation and Internment of Civilians to reassess U.S. policies toward Japanese Americans during WWII. The commission's report, published in 1983, found that there was no "military necessity" for the internment of Japanese Americans, and that the historical causes for it were "race prejudice, war hysteria, and a failure of political leadership." For more than two decades, Japanese American advocacy groups struggled for compensation and an acknowledgment of wrongdoing from the government. The Civil Liberties Act of 1988, signed by President Ronald Reagan, provided an apology from the U.S. government and an individual payment of $20,000 (about $50,000 in 2009 dollars) to 60,000 surviving internees.

U.S. Aid to Post WWII Europe

The European Recovery Program (ERP) was a United States program of financial assistance to help rebuild European nations devastated by World War II. After the war, Europe's agricultural and coal production had nearly stopped, and its people were threatened with starvation. The United States responded and, after careful planning, announced in June 1947 that if Europe devised a cooperative, long-term rebuilding program, the United States would provide funding.

The program is also known as the Marshall Plan and is the subject of a Library exhibition called "For European Recovery: The Fiftieth Anniversary of the Marshall Plan." Under the program, the United States provided aid to prevent starvation in the major war areas, repair the devastation of those areas as quickly as possible and begin economic reconstruction. The plan had two major aims: (1) preventing the spread of communism in Western Europe and (2) stabilizing the international order to favor development of political democracies and free-market economies.

During the four years in which the Marshall Plan was formally in operation, Congress appropriated $13.3 billion, which represents more than $120 billion today.

Source: USAID From The American People *http://www.usaid.gov*

Post World War II Assistance to Germany

United States assistance to Germany totaled $4.3 billion ($39 billion in 2009 dollars) for the years of direct military government (May 1945-May 1949) and the overlapping Marshall Plan years (1949-1952). Initial funding, primarily under the Government and Relief in Occupied Areas (GARIOA) program, was directed primarily at humanitarian relief. GARIOA provided funding for the basic relief supplies necessary for "the prevention of disease and unrest prejudicial to the occupying forces" and was limited to food, fertilizers, seed, and minimum petroleum requirements. The Marshall Plan provided a third of total United States aid to Germany. It provided the first funding for Germany with the specific objective of promoting economic recovery. The official figure for total Marshall Plan assistance to Germany is about $1.4 billion in current-year dollars $12.7 billion in 2009 dollars, of which $9.9 billion was grants and $2.8 billion was loans. The entire amount of Marshall Plan aid is usually considered economic reconstruction funding.

Source: USAID From The American People *http://www.usaid.gov*

Post World War II Assistance to Japan

Total U.S. assistance to Japan for the years of U.S. occupation, from 1946–1952, was $2.2 billion ($20 billion in 2009 dollars), of which almost $1.7 billion were grants and $504 million was loans. There is no readily available published information regarding how much of this was provided for economic reconstruction, although the intent of the occupation after 1948 was to promote economic recovery. The total value of U.S. aid from the occupation is just slightly over $20 billion in current dollars. A significant part of this money went to assistance for industrial capital formation and rebuilding Japan's factories. This consisted of funding for industrial machinery and parts, vehicles and motor parts, and related miscellaneous equipment and supplies.

Some of U.S. funding went to categories that would contribute directly to economic reconstruction, i.e., industrial materials, machinery, petroleum, vehicles, and equipment. Some funding established payment to civilians, which was considered to be contributing to economic reconstruction, especially as Japanese labor was provided incentives in order to encourage production. The total in 2009 dollars for these payments to civilians and miscellaneous was approximately $1.25 billion. The various categories of aid totaled $6.8 billion in 2009 dollars. Of an additional $1.2 billion, $1.19 billion went to agricultural equipment, foodstuffs, and food supplies. This was aimed at helping to feed the Japanese population. The remainder was expenditures for medical supplies, education, clothing, textiles, and shoes.

Source: USAID From The American People *http://www.usaid.gov*

U.S. Aid to Israel

The United States extended recognition to the state of Israel on May 14, 1948. President Truman recognized the state of Israel on January 31, 1949. At the time, U.S. foreign policy was geared toward supporting the development of oil-producing countries while maintaining a neutral stance in the Arab-Israeli conflict. U.S. policymakers used foreign aid in the 1950s and 1960s to support these objectives. U.S. Direct aid to Israel from 1949 to 2000 was approximately $78 billion.

Appropriations bills for FY 2001, which began October 1, 2000, included, in addition to the $2.82 billion in economic and military foreign aid to Israel, an additional $60 million in refugee resettlement and $250 million in the DOD budget, plus $85 million interest, for a total of at least $3.2 billion. In addition, on November 14, 2000, President Clinton sent a special request to Congress for an additional $450 million in military aid to Israel in FY 2001, plus $350 million for FY 2002.

Israel now receives about 3 billion dollars in direct foreign assistance each year, an amount that is roughly one-sixth of America's direct foreign assistance budget. In addition to $81.3 billion through FY 2000, there was $4.3 billion from the DOD, $1.7 billion in interest from disbursement of aid, and $3.2 billion in other categories, giving a grand total of $90.6 billion total aid to Israel through FY 2001. Approval of Clinton's special request for $450 million in military aid pushed the number over $91 billion in FY 2002 U.S. Direct aid to Israel from 2003 through 2008 was approximately $15 billion bringing total aid to Israel to approximately $104 billion in 2008.

Source: Washington Report on Middle East Affairs
USAID From The American People *http://www.usaid.gov*

U.S. Aid to IRAQ

From 2003 to 2006, Congress approved $30 billion for large-scale rebuilding projects in Iraq while the United States shifted its focus to providing the training and tools Iraqis need to govern themselves.

In a quarterly report to Congress, Special Inspector General for Iraq Reconstruction, Stuart Bowen, described 2008 as a "year of transfer" in Iraq. The report says the United States has spent about 90 percent of a fund created by Congress in 2003 for public-works projects, such as electrical-generating stations and health clinics.

There is a separate fund for projects that teach Iraqi officials how to self-govern and manage its affairs. Less than 20 percent of that fund, a $3.3 billion account, supplies tools such as computers and software, and President Bush's 2009 budget proposal contained another $400 million for additional support.

The U.S. State, Defense, and Treasury departments are funding training programs for officials at Iraqi ministries to teach Iraqis how to plan and implement budgets, buy goods and services, and manage employees.

U.S. assistance to Iraq appropriated from FY2003 to FY2006 totaled $28.9 billion. All of it is grant assistance. While most funds were appropriated to a special Iraq Relief and Reconstruction Fund (IRRF, $21 billion) and an Iraq Security Forces Fund ($5.7 billion), additional sums from the budgets of DOD and other agencies have been used for reconstruction purposes. The Departments of State and Defense as well as USAID are the key entities responsible for implementing Iraq assistance programs. Nearly 40 percent of total funding, about $11.5 billion, was targeted for restoring economically critical infrastructure, including airports, roads, bridges, railroads, seaports, electric power, water and sanitation, telecommunications, and essential buildings. An additional $6.2 billion was allocated to assist democratization, education and health, and the expansion of the private sector.

Together, the infrastructure reconstruction assistance, which best corresponds to the bulk of aid provided to Germany and Japan, and the social, economic, and political development aid which is more characteristic of current U.S. assistance around the world, make up nearly two-thirds of total Iraq funding for economic and political reconstruction to date.

Source: Washington Report on Middle East Affairs
            USAID From The American People *http://www.usaid.gov*

U.S. Aid to Afghanistan

From 2002-2009, USAID invested a total of $9B in Afghanistan with 32.6 percent and 32.3 percent going to people and economic growth respectively. The money was invested for the following objectives:

COST OF OPERATIONS (Dollars *in Thousands*)
$1,386,054 (14.9%) for Humanitarian Assistance
$3,029,681 (32.6%) for Investing in People
$3,000,895 (32.3%) for Economic Growth
$1,303,047 (14.0%) for Governing and Democracy
$117,152 (1.3%) for Unit management
$459,065 (4.9%) for Peace and Security

Supplies: USAID provided wool blankets, quilts, shelter kits, sheet, tents, mattresses, clothes, stoves, cooking sets, firewood, coal, lanterns, and water containers.

Health care: USAID provided medical kits and funds for health centers and mobile clinics.

Housing: USAID performed small scale spot reconstruction, providing materials to rehabilitate damaged housing for returning displaced persons.

Roads: USAID is providing funds to upgrade and rebuild roads, especially to markets, and repair and reconstruct bridges.

Water Systems: USAID is paying for the drilling of wells, the construction and repair of irrigation and water-supply systems, and the operation and maintenance of water pumping systems to provide people with potable water.

Agriculture: USAID provided $13 million (7,000 metric tons) of seed, fertilizer and technical assistance to 40,000 farmers.

Source: Washington Report on Middle East Affairs
USAID From The American People *http://www.usaid.gov*

Bibliography

1. Malcolm Gladwell, Outliers: The Story of Success (Little Brown and Company, 2008)
2. Cartwright, Samuel. 1851. "Diseases and Peculiarities of the Negro Race," *DeBow's Review*. (Southern and Western States: New Orleans), Volume XI.
3. The Gallup Organization, Gallup Poll Social Audit, 2001. Black-White Relations in the United States, 2001 Update, July 10: 7-9.
4. The Gallup Organization, Gallup Poll, #761, May, 1968
5. "How Whites Feel About Negroes: A Painful American Dilemma," Newsweek, October 21, 1963: 56
6. The Gallup Organization, Gallup Poll #699, October, 1964
7. Newsweek/Gallup Organization, National Opinion Survey, August 19, 1969
8. Ford, Glen and Peter Campbell, 2006. "Katrina: A Study-Black Consensus, White Dispute." The Black Commentator, Issue 165, January 5
9. W. E. B. Dubois, Souls of Black Folks (Chicago: A.C McClurg & Co.,1903)
10. DuBois, W. E. B., Black Reconstruction in America, 1860-1880 (Free Press, 1999)
11. Foner, Eric, Reconstruction: America's Unfinished Revolution, 1863-1877 (New York: Harper Perennial, 2002)
12. Rosen, Louis, The South Side: The Racial Transformation of an American Neighborhood (Chicago: ivan R. Dee, 1999)
13. Davis, David Brion, The Problem of Slavery in Western Culture (Ithaca: Cornell University Press, 1966)
14. Kolchin, Peter, American Slavery: 1619-1877 (London and New York: Penguin, 1995)

15. Curtin, Phillip D, The Atlantic Slave Trade: A Census (Madison: University of Wisconsin Press, 1969)
16. Reynolds, Edward, Stand the Storm: A History of the Atlantic Slave Trade (London: Allison and Busby, 1985)
17. Bender, Thomas, ed., The Antislavery Debate: Capitalism and Abolitionism as a Problem in Historical Interpretation (Oxford: University of California Press, 1992)
18. Free, Jr., Marvin D., African Americans and the Criminal Justice System (Taylor & Francis, 1992)
19. Curry, George E., The Affirmative Action Debate (Perseus Books, 1996)
20. Dierenfield, Bruce J., The Civil Rights Movement (Great Britain: Pearsoned, 2004, 2008)
21. Lommel, Cookie, The History of Rap Music (Chelsea House Publications, May 2001)
22. *Claude M. Steele, The Atlantic Monthly, August 1999 Thin Ice: Stereotype Threat and Black College Students*
23. Steele, C. M. (1997). A threat in the air: How stereotypes shape the intellectual identities and performance of women and African-Americans. *American Psychologist*
24. Steele, C. M. (1999) Thin ice: "Stereotype threat" and Black college students. *The Atlantic Monthly*, August, *http://www.theatlantic.com/doc/199908/student-stereotype*
25. Steele, C. M., & Aronson, J. (1995). Stereotype threat and the intellectual test performance of African-Americans. *Journal of Personality and Social Psychology*
26 USAID From The American People *http://www.usaid.gov*
27. The Shape of the River, Bok, Derek and Bowen, William G., September, 1998
28. The Federal Glass Ceiling Commission Report, December, 1995
29. The Census Bureau, Statistical Abstract of the United States, 1996
30. The U.S. Department of Labor, Women's Bureau, September, 1996
31. Black Americans in Defense of Our Nation, the Office of the Deputy Assistant Secretary of Defense for Civilian Personnel Policy and Equal Opportunity, 1991

Index

U

V

W

7254180R0

Made in the USA
Lexington, KY
03 November 2010